Lisbon

...

A guide to recent architecture

Paulo Santos

Lisbon

A guide to recent architecture

●●● ellipsis KÖNEMANN

•••

CREATED, EDITED AND DESIGNED BY
Ellipsis London Limited
2 Rufus Street London N1 6PE
E MAIL ...@ellipsis.co.uk
WWW http://www.ellipsis.com
PUBLISHED IN THE UK AND AFRICA BY
Ellipsis London Limited
SERIES EDITOR Tom Neville
SERIES DESIGN Jonathan Moberly

COPYRIGHT © 1998 Könemann
Verlagsgesellschaft mbH
Bonner Str. 126, D-50968 Köln
PRODUCTION MANAGER Detlev Schaper
PRINTING AND BINDING Sing Cheong
Printing Ltd
Printed in Hong Kong

ISBN 3 8290 0473 7 (Könemann)
ISBN 1 899858 62 8 (Ellipsis)

Paulo Santos 1998

Contents

Introduction 6

Using this book 10

Baixa to Chiado 13

Restauradores to Parque Eduardo VII 57

Amoreiras to Campolide 87

Alges, Belém and Santo Amaro 107

Saldanha to Arieiro 129

Cidade Universitária 151

Benfica 167

Olaias to Olivais 185

Parque Expo 205

Index 229

Introduction

Long gone are the days when Portugal literally was brought to its knees, both economically and culturally, by Salazar's dictatorial rule. Antonio de Oliveira Salazar ruled Portugal for more than 40 years as dictator. He came to power in 1932 after a military coup. It was another military coup, on 25 April 1974, that was to free Portugal and bring it democracy.

As prime minister, then as president, Salazar's first priority was to modernise the Portuguese armed forces, followed by improvements to infrastructure and telecommunications in the country's major cities – the countryside was ignored completely. Salazar also saw it as a duty to rebuild the Portuguese overseas empire, which had collapsed after a decade of colonial wars.

As a dictator he was unique, the most fastidious and private of this century's dictators in Europe. Lacking in charisma and with no interest in self publicity, he preferred the solace and comfort of his home.

Salazar died in 1970, two years after being replaced as president by Marcello Caetano. It was Caetano's brief dictatorship that was overthrown in 1974 by the Armed Forces Movement, led by General Spinola, finally ending totalitarianism in Portugal.

The Salazar government's overt concern with heritage, restoring only the more prestigious historic monuments, led to the neglect and disfigurement of Lisbon's urban fabric. Subsequently the democratic state reintroduced urban-restoration plans for areas in critical need, but they have had to be postponed repeatedly.

In recent years Lisbon has undergone a complete transformation with many new buildings and building types appearing from the smallest of designs to the largest infrastructure projects. In essence, the traditional architectural models and nostalgia for the past have been left behind as the country plunges into the future, just as the discoverer of the sea route to India, Vasco da Gama, did more than 500 years ago. What has caused this transformation? Antonio Guterres, the socialist prime minister, has played an important part in the country's economic resurgence and renewed cultural development, funded in large part by the European Community. The figures speak for themselves: an economic growth rate of 4 per cent, a sharp drop in inflation to 3 per cent (down 1 per cent in a year), a boom in private consumption and public expenditures of 2 per cent, and an increase in fixed investments of 6.5 per cent. The resulting expansion in the services' sector has also created a boom in the real-estate market, both in the city and along the coast.

Although already a member of the European Community, the economic expansion is bringing Portugal on a par with other member states, and it is this optimism for the future well-being of the country that is encapsulated in the current investment and enthusiasm for Portugal's architectural and cultural showcase – Expo 98. The exposition will be more than just a commemorative event. It is a deeply entrenched project designed to project Lisbon into the next millennium. Expo displays a new architectural bravura inspired by many new and young practices with fresh approaches to architecture. The opportunities for architectural work were limited several years ago and commissions were normally awarded to bigger and more renowned conservative practices. However, membership of the European Community has transformed Portuguese architectural practice by introducing the concept of architectural competitions and proposals – changes in the rules have allowed smaller firms to compete in all areas of construction and have fuelled the current rise in Lisbon's architectural fortunes.

The overall effect on architecture has been immense, and promising developments in the infrastructure of the city are currently being built.

Lisbon: a guide to recent architecture

For example, the 25 de Abril bridge, originally built in 1966 and designed to carry a railway line (but until now not a financially viable option), will connect the periphery south of the centre with the rest of the city, making it more accessible and commercially prosperous. The new 15-km Vasco da Gama bridge will connect the Expo site to the country and will provide easier routes both north and south while avoiding the heart of Lisbon. There will also be direct access with the airport. A series of new express-ways around the north of the city, ferry terminals and train stations, and the Expo site, will be built by 1998. The Chiado link will be designed by Alvaro Siza Vieira, while the more ambitious Metro City by Tomás Taveira is yet to be realised.

Housing is also on the rise and will be integrated with the city fabric. Previously housing was planned around the city's periphery. Since its autonomy from the municipality in 1994, the Departamento de Construção de Habitação, or Department for Housing Construction, has received new independent status and can now commission better housing. Sadly, applications for funding are often slow or delayed and the city is still witnessing the completion of building projects commissioned before 1994. A few luxury apartment blocks are being constructed in the city centre to encourage population growth in the area. A survey in 1990 showed that Lisbon had less than 700,000 inhabitants because of the availability of cheaper housing in the suburbs.

The architecture of education is also on the rise. University colleges are expanding and, although the Technical University has its own archi-tectural department, it is not unusual for competitions to be held to encourage foreign styles and influences. The Faculty of Veterinary Sciences promises to be a spectacular building as does the Institute of Management and Economy by Gonçalo Byrne.

Public architecture is also increasing. Ricardo Bofill, designer of Barcelona airport in Spain, also works in Lisbon with his usual palette based on a transparent classical box, while on the Expo site BDP are currently designing a shopping centre with two sail-like towers (due to open in 1999). Lisbon's green spaces will also be improved and renovated with a planned project to create a better urban environment, the provision of many pedestrianised areas and an extension to the Parque Eduardo VII to give the best panoramic view of the city. Currently, the most important work is the restoration of the Chiado by Siza. The project was started in 1988 and has already won an award for the work in progress.

As outlined above, the book was an opportunity to investigate both the culture and architecture of a city of which I had no true prior knowledge. I was born in Lisbon, but had left at an early age. Besides getting to know architects and other professionals, it was yet another chance to develop professionally and personally. I make no claims, however, to being an expert in what is evolving around the city. My notes derive from what I saw and by what was being justified by the those in the know and those directly involved with projects.

NOTE: The Secil Architectural Prize was founded in 1992 by the Secil cement company. The Portuguese Architectural Association awards the prize of £20,000 biennially to works of special architectural merit that have used cement in their construction. The award goes to major public works, such as schools, libraries, museums and theatres.

Using this book

The aim of the guide is to introduce Lisbon's architectural development over the past 10 years by means of a tour of some of the more recent building types in its up-and-coming and exciting districts.

The guide is divided into nine sections, each covering an area with buildings of interest. Most buildings can be reached on foot and details of how to do so are under each entry. The site's address has map coordinates that refer to the *Extra* edition map by Falkplan. Public transport other than the metro is not particularly good. Buses are often uncomfortable, while the new trams are great to travel in but are not frequent. The metro, on the other hand, is best outside the rush hour. The Portuguese are often well informed about new places and are always keen to assist, though I suggest caution if visiting the Bairros social housing which is not always safe.

ACKNOWLEDGEMENTS
I thank all the architects, journalists and clients that I have been involved with for being so helpful, especially to: Raul de Carvalho, for many contacts; Luis Trigueiros and Michel Toussaint for pointing me in the right direction and so kindly assisting with my buildings' list; the Pedrosas for providing sustenance; Louise for help and encouragement; Tom Neville, the publisher, for making the book possible; Patrick Hannay for being my mentor; and Jude for all her loving support.
PS March 1998

1 Baixa to Chiado
2 Restauradores to Parque Eduardo VII
3 Amoreiras to Campolide
4 Alges, Belém and Santo Amaro
5 Saldanha to Arieiro
6 Cidade Universitária
7 Benfica
8 Olaias to Olivais
9 Parque Expo

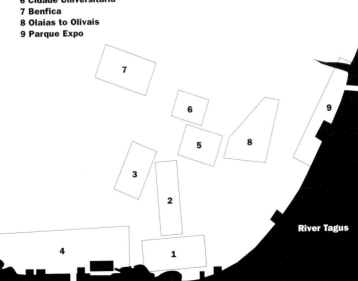

Baixa to Chiado

Dona Maria II National Theatre: bookshop, bar and ticket office   14

Bandarra shoe shop   18

i Kiosk   20

Archaeological Nucleus Museum   22

Espaço OIKOS   26

Ana Salazar shop   30

Chiado restructuring and the Castro & Melo building   34

Atalaia 31 shop   38

Café Targus   40

Casanostra restaurant   42

Patine shop   44

Consenso restaurant   46

Museum of Contemporary Art   48

Portuguese Architects Association   52

Dona Maria II National Theatre: bookshop, bar and ticket office

Entered directly from the street or through the restrained grandeur of the theatre, this small bookshop is consumed by a modern sculptural installation that houses a collection of theatre and arts-related material and which defines the remaining space. Enclosed by thick, rich, timber shelving on the surrounding walls, this cubic furniture element, with its minimal detailing, makes interesting use of the limited space by also providing a second level, reached by a staircase formed by the shelving beneath. With its slim, metal shelves, the 'bookcase' appears as a delicate insertion to which the weight of the books adds volume. The structure allows the upper parts of the walls to remain bare and to be a part of the white ceiling, which serves to open the space. A tall, cylindrical pole topped by a circular marble plate is lit from above and glows with a soft, warm light, appearing to anchor the balcony overhead.

The bookshop is one of three obviously modern elements introduced to the theatre since its reconstruction in 1964. Yet another victim of fire, the theatre's exterior façades and east atrium were all that was kept of the original building. To either side of the imposing historical façade of the main entrance are glazed insertions that close the arcades of the old building and project internal spaces into the exterior.

Tucked away to one side, the monochrome grey-polished stone of the bar area maintains the solidity of the original structure without imitating it. Modern chairs and tables spill out into the glazed arcade from where the activity around the train station opposite can be viewed in an atmosphere of quiet elegance. The simple reception and ticket desks with their menacing glass fins are carefully inserted between columns and form an entrance to the bookshop.

Gonçalo Byrne 1994

Gonçalo Byrne 1994

The theatre itself is inaccessible except during performances. However, obtaining a ticket for the toilets from the bar provides an opportunity to view the interior splendour *en route*.

ADDRESS Praça D Pedro IV, Rossio [2N]
METRO Rossio
ACCESS opens at 10.00

Gonçalo Byrne 1994

Gonçalo Byrne 1994

Baixa to Chiado

Bandarra shoe shop

Bandarra is a chain of shoe shops that caters for the younger generation. By skilfully abstracting the traditional ways and concepts of displaying the shoe in its shops, Bandarra creates a dramatic but responsive exhibit from the displays. Shoes are arranged on a limestone plinth running around the perimeter of the shop, and interrupted only by the entrance. This surface is the only display area for the footwear, sustaining the concept of the items being part of the display. It also allows only a limited number of customers at any given time in the relatively small, rectangular space.

The aim, therefore, is to exploit and express the product throughout its setting, a goal achieved with a rustic grey and ochre palette, and a self-contained staircase which transforms itself from a straight run to an elegant spiral, disappearing into the ceiling. The entire design is a bold and considered attempt to create an atmosphere in keeping with the times.

There are other Bandarras by Beitão at Olivais Sul shopping centre, shop 108 [9T], and on Avenida Roma 55-B [70].

ADDRESS Rua Sta Justa 78 [2N]
METRO Rossio
ACCESS 10.00–18.00

J Nuno Beitão 1991

J Nuno Beitão 1991

i Kiosk

A recent newcomer to Lisbon's streets is this simple, quaint information stand. Nomadic by nature, it has been sighted sporting an 'i' symbol billowing in the wind above its four sails which shelter its rectilinear, black figure from the sun's heat. The kiosk is beyond being a sculptural form and is more likely a lucid, slender box assuming a strange and magical quality. An ubiquitous form in various styles in the city, each dealing with its own peculiarity, this one happens to deal out information, free! A friendly gesture from a small but magnanimous country.

ADDRESS scattered throughout Lisbon, last seen on Rua Augusta [1C, 1N]
CLIENT Lisboa Card, Camâra Municipal de Lisboa (CML)
SUPPLIERS AND CONSTRUCTION Larus, LDA
COST £3500
SIZE 2 X 1.3 X 2.6 metres
METRO Rossio
ACCESS 10.00–19.00

Jorge Moleirinho 1997

Jorge Moleirinho 1997

Archaeological Nucleus Museum

The Portuguese Commercial Bank commands an inspiring site facing the pedestrianised Rua Augusta in the Baixa (downtown). It is housed in a late eighteenth-century Pombalino structure, which relates to a rigorous and gridded town plan, based on French principles but modelled on London and Turin, devised by Eugenio dos Santos and promptly favoured and executed by the Marques de Pombal. This methodical plan submerged and covered the area, completely destroyed by the disastrous earthquake of 1775.

The Nucleus was created after Roman ruins of the third and fourth centuries AD and Moorish remains were discovered during the remodelling and extension of the Portuguese Commercial Bank's headquarters. The museum modestly occupies two display rooms and a basement, which extends under two of six modified buildings. The overall design is carried through an administration department, an international office, two public banking departments and the museum itself. The project is an exercise in detailing while simultaneously bringing out the qualities of the old buildings.

Initially visitors gather at the Rua dos Correeiros reception, which is clad in a smooth limestone that merges amiably with the old Pombalino arched ceiling, supported by rough but elegant stone columns. The foundation of one of the columns is exposed by glass inset at an angle in the dark granite floor. The opportunity to display the found articles arises in a separate bay from the reception area. Here the floor is completely made of glass and extends to a third room to expose a drum used by the Romans to contain and store fish, within a wall surrounding the decaying remains of a mosaic floor.

The detailing is simple, clear and elegant. This is carried over to the treatment of the basement where access is through the second room. A

Intergaup 1994–95

Baixa to Chiado

suspended steel walkway reinforces the transparency of the floor surfaces above, weaving through dark chambers, occasionally showing views of the functioning bank above through glazed floors.

ADDRESS Rua dos Correeiros 9 [IN]
CLIENT Banco Commercial Português
SIZE 8334 square metres
METRO Rossio
TRAM 28 to Rua do Comercio
ACCESS limited numbers, book at door; Thursday 15.00–17.00, Saturday
10.00–12.30, 14.30–16.30

Intergaup 1994–95

Intergaup 1994–95

Espaço OIKOS

Espaço OIKOS is an ethnographic organisation which seeks to develop an awareness of the cultural heritage of the Portuguese, specifically that involving its previously underdeveloped colonies, by using exhibitions, concerts, talks, etc. Located below the Castle de São Jorge in Alfama, a tenth-century Muslim fort, the Espaço houses temporary exhibitions of artefacts drawn mainly from the cultures of Portugal's former African colonies.

OIKOS occupies a vast hall contained under graceful arches of brick and stone, and has an extraordinary array of individual troughs which recall the hall's former use as a stable for the archbishop of the nearby Sé. The hall has been impressively transformed into an awe-inspiring, temple-like space, with each trough individually lit, dramatising its contained displays. The floor is dressed in an uneven stone surface that had to be raised and replaced due to the discovery of a third-century AD Roman theatre below.

The vaulted Espaço is sited at one end of the vast hall, like a house within a house, maintaing its autonomy. The covered top section is reserved for the more private and contained administration, but below it is subdivided into an open and public space.

The only disruption to the original building is the inclusion of the toilets in a chamber that was previously used by vehicles as the entrance to the building when it was occupied by the PIDE (the secret police of the dictatorial government prior to 1974). Now it is discreetly enclosed and restored with a sliding door and is situated below the stairs.

The display area uses steel columns, wooden floors and corrugated sheets as wall surfaces. Also in the same materials are a bar, several tables and a display unit which is part of a sliding door designed to maximise its area and creating a storage space behind. This display area is set on

Rui Pedro Cabrita and Miguel Ângelo Silva 1991–93

Rui Pedro Cabrita and Miguel Ângelo Silva 1991–93

a platform rather like a viewing stage for the objects within the vast open space of the gallery.

ADDRESS Rua Augusto Rosa 40 [10]
TRAM 28 from Rua do Comercio
BUS 37 from Estação cais do Sodré
ACCESS 10.00–18.00

Rui Pedro Cabrita and Miguel Ângelo Silva 1991–93

Baixa to Chiado

Rui Pedro Cabrita and Miguel Ângelo Silva 1991–93

Ana Salazar shop

Ana Salazar is probably one of the best-known women's fashion designers in Portugal. She has shops scattered around Lisbon and, until recently, one in Paris. Her main shop is at the bottom end of the Chiado, in the prominent Rua do Carmo, renowned as one of the city's most elegant shopping streets. The shop was affected by building work on the Metro's new extension and the stations between the Restauradores, Chiado and Cais Sodre. Unsurprisingly, dust and noise made it impossible to work within, and the owner was quick to set up a temporary store close by.

The result is an insertion occupying a double-height space as part of the restructured Chiado (see page 34) and which retains the rough exposed cement render. This is a common finish in most of the commercial interiors in the new area, allowing tenants to interfere with the space as they want.

Facing the tall and slender street doors and windows is a wood-studded divide of deep fuchsia that carries the shop's delicate logo and forms a canvas for two modern chandeliers made of a simple ring with several oval-shaped light bulbs suspended on fine wires. This ensemble complements well the cash till and clothes racks that exaggerate a raucous design, not only by echoing the interior with its cement render, but also by highlighting its ephemerality.

In early 1998 the main store (Rua do Carmo 87 [2N]) reopened after being completely remodelled. It lacks the openness and expressive detail, exposing all its nuts and bolts, of the first and most popular store. The remodelled store is more simple and enclosed, floodlit with artificial lighting from a completely glazed but frosted ceiling, and partitioned with planes which give the interior a look related to the current revival of 1960s' modernism. The clothes appear to be invigortaed by the sheer

Manuel Graça Dias and Egas José Vieira 1996

quantity of light, as if on show on a catwalk.

There is an earlier Salazar shop by Dias and Vieira on Avenida Roma 16-E [70].

ADDRESS Rua Nova da Almada 89 [1N]
METRO Rossio or Chiado
ACCESS 10.00–18.00

Manuel Graça Dias and Egas José Vieira 1996

Manuel Graça Dias and Egas José Vieira 1996

Chiado restructuring and the Castro & Melo building

In August 1988 a fire broke out in the Chiado, burning down a part of one of Lisbon's oldest quarters. The Municipal Administration (at the time headed by the engineer Nuno Abecassis) appealed for aid, and France, with the Grands Projets, offered assistance. Subsequently, Alvaro Siza Vieira was asked to initiate a detailed plan for the reconstruction of the area. Accordingly, the Chiado's Recovery Department oversaw general coordination, provided technical advice on the restoration of the original façades and integrated the Municipal's Plan for the whole city (Plano Director) with the Baixa Urban Renewal in keeping with the area's environmental, historical and architectonic values.

The Chiado is a transition zone between the city's Baixa or downtown, an urban area designed and constructed by the Marques de Pombal following the earthquake of 1755, and the Bairro Alto, the capital's bohemian district, which is the most important civic and commercial space in the city.

Here, between these two striking neighbourhoods, the Rua do Carmo rises, passing beneath the famous Santa Justa elevator, to the ruins of the Chiado. Some buildings are still hidden behind hoardings. The fire mainly affected the Rua do Camo, Rua Nova da Almada and Rua Garret, and it is here that the restructuring is most visible with retailers already taking up residence.

The architectural response concentrates on the area as a whole rather than on individual buildings, i.e. the architectural merit comes less from the quality of the buildings than from the manner in which they structure and reinforce the shape of the city. Hence, new public walkways, once blocked by gates, have reappeared and surprise pathways lead to courtyards with calm, serene spaces pleasantly contrasting with the tumult of

Alvaro Siza Vieira 1991–94

the streets.

The Castro & Melo building, originally a Pombaline structure, is recognisable by its austere and serene, narrow balconies with flat façades, often dressed in colours distinctive of the period, i.e. either light yellow, blue or red. Even though the building was completely rebuilt, a precise but discreet attention to detail, which is characteristic of the architect, provides an apparent simplicity reflecting the Pombaline age. The building was remodelled for residential use leaving the ground floor for shops. On the inside, the upper apartment floors are simple in detail and are noteworthy for their lucid and sober spirit. Although the building now has an unmistakably modern idiom, it complements and maintains the historical image.

ADDRESS Rua Nova da Almada 95 [1N]
CLIENT Camãra Municipal de Lisboa (CML)
ENGINEER STA Segadaes Tavares Associados, LDA
CONTRACT VALUE about £250 million
SIZE 570 square metres
METRO Chiado or Rossio
ACCESS none, visible from the street
Secil Architecture Prize 1996

Baixa to Chiado

Alvaro Siza Vieira 1991–94

Baixa to Chiado

Alvaro Siza Vieira 1991–94

Atalaia 31 shop

In 1988, to coincide with the Chiado restructuring, the Bairro Alto Department was formed, its aim to renovate the much-neglected historic hill district of the Bairro Alto. Progress has been slow over the past decade, but recently the neighbourhood has undergone a vast improvement, mainly due to the number of visitors expected for the Expo.

Atalaia 31 is a single-storey shop selling men's clothes. It is self contained and divorced from the rundown area of Bairro Alto by its distinctive design of simplicity and openness. Inside, one wall cut by geometric pools of glass stands opposite the reception counter in a space roughly rectangular and bound by a mix of soothing green and burgundy walls. Display cabinets are contained around the perimeter and echo in their materials dark-stained wood. The large, sweeping curve of the counter is designed to extend in the rectangular space and has behind it an area for a private office and a changing room.

Baixa to Chiado

ADDRESS Rua da Atalaia 31 [2M]
CLIENT 3100 Confeções e Brindes, LDA
TRAM 28 to Praça L Camoês
ACCESS open

Antonio Lagarto 1993

Antonio Lagarto 1993

Café Targus

Part of the capital's vitality is the Olisipeans' passion for bars. Many are being built in the fabric of the city by a new generation of architects as well as designers. The Café Targus is in the Bairro Alto, the higher quarter of the city, which by day is a small, grubby residential area overflowing with commercial vans, but by night is full of vivacious and abundant restaurants, and bars full of lively conversation, wine and *bica* (espresso). Needless to say, the Targus is popular with architects, journalists, writers, painters and like-minded professionals.

During the day the double doors of the entrance are opened giving an unhindered and welcoming view of the street. At night, however, entry is through a single-leaf opening that leads to an unsuccessfully designed cloak cupboard (it is intended to make this small space a cigar dispensary). The bar stands somewhat apart by its use of pure forms and surfaces. It is separated from the rest of the café by lustrous fins covered in gold mosaics yet at the same time is linked to it by a tapering screen which sweeps across to conceal the lavatories and the kitchen to the rear.

The café holds exhibitions of the work of young, local painters and plans are underway to extend it next door to create the Targus Classico.

ADDRESS Rua Diario Noticias, 40B [2M]
CLIENT Hernam Miguel
SIZE 115 square metres
TRAM 28 to Praça L Camo's then walk up to Rua do Norte
ACCESS 12.00–03.00

Maria Manuel von Half and Mario Soledade Sousa 1990

Maria Manuel von Half and Mario Soledade Sousa 1990

Casanostra restaurant

Casanostra is not a new Italian restaurant, being 12 years old, but the latest addition by Manuel Graça Dias and Egas José Vieira has added a concealed enclosure. The signs of wear and tear in the restaurant have been left as is. The original decor is a distinctive palette of mint and cream with an ornate pattern of electrical leads displaying a criss-cross arrangement on the ceiling.

There is, however, an uneasiness between the old and new parts of the restaurant. The new extension is necessarily self-contained and has a certain quirkiness about it, especially the astonishing colours used on each wall, namely a bright orange with spikes placed precariously on it on one side; and on the other side a cross of blue and red, with a spinning dumbwaiter and linen-drawer inset. The restaurant has a particular brand of informality, intimacy and good food, all consumed in flamboyant surroundings, and it is this which makes it a popular place for revellers.

Baixa to Chiado

ADDRESS Travessa do Poço da Cidade 60 [2M]
CLIENT Maria Paola Porru
TRAM 28 to Praça L Camões then to Rua Atalaia
ACCESS Tuesday–Sunday 12.00–15.00, 19.00–01.00

Manuel Graça Dias and Egas José Vieira 1996

Manuel Graça Dias and Egas José Vieira 1996

Patine shop

Patine is an extremely small and tight space with little to intervene in its interior other than a long, bench-like table which stretches out to welcome you at the entrance. The shop displays an array of internationally renowned *couture* that appears too delicate in its surroundings. The shop was designed exclusively to deal with the night life so typical of this area, a fact reminiscent in its grubby surroundings and suggested by its rustic logo.

ADDRESS Travessa Água da Flor 32, Bairro Alto [2M]
CLIENT J P F P da Silva
TRAM 28 to Praça L Camoês then to Rua Atalaia
ACCESS 14.00–midnight

Antonio Meira 1996

Consenso restaurant

On entering the Consenso restaurant, a glass sheet shields the bar from the street and once off the carpeted stairs you notice the steel flooring. The bar, used as a waiting area before dining, has a floor with a glazed-grid light source illuminating the space beneath the vaults. Separating the dining area and the bar is an office and the lavatories, the latter being simply an array of framed mirrors that act as partitions to create a dramatic chamber from what is normally a fatuous space. Further on, three dining rooms act as galleries with murals on facing walls. The final room is used for special clients and its orderly walls and ceiling of brick and stone are hidden intermittently by an angled plaster surface decorated with flowers. Light, as in the bar area, is uniform along the periphery and is set below glass and wrought-iron rods.

All in all, the restaurant's rich and varied design constantly dramatises the series of rooms made in the fabric of the old building.

Baixa to Chiado

ADDRESS Rua da Academia
das Ciências 1-1A [2M]
CLIENT Siedik Karim
TRAM 28 to Calçada do Combro,
then walk up Rua do Seculo
ACCESS daily except Sunday

Paulo Lugero de Castro 1994

Paulo Lugero de Castro 1994

Museum of Contemporary Art

As part of the programme of reconstruction in the central Chiado district, French architect Jean-Michel Wilmotte was commissioned by the Portuguese Cultural Heritage Institute to reorganise and enlarge the existing Portuguese National Museum of Contemporary Art, renamed the Chiado National Gallery. Established in 1911 within the walls of the former eighteenth-century San Francisco Convent, it now houses a collection of art from the mid-nineteenth century to the present day, together with a bookshop, café and terraced garden.

The solid, bare walls of the exterior provide few clues about the treasures within; a glimpse of the garden through a barred entrance way and a banner reveal the museum's existence. Relying on the depth of the walls to create the division between street and gallery, a glazed partition is the only barrier when passing through the dramatic vaulted entrance hall. The rustic stone columns and brick arches immediately betray the building as a former warehouse and bakery built after the earthquake of 1755. A wall of traditional brick ovens, carefully restored, is further evidence and creates an interesting display in the temporary exhibition area. On the floor above, their distinctive chimneys break through the skyline. Wilmotte's intervention rests lightly on the existing structure allowing not only modern and traditional styles to speak independently, but also the demonstration of an interior architecture where contrasting elements coexist and enhance one another with the clean, modern lines providing an eloquent contrast with the gentle curves of the sculptures and arches; the subdued colours of the galleries against the ornate gilt frames and opulence of former centuries; and the suspended metal staircase and footbridges held within the historic framework of the existing structure.

The old museum originally extended from the convent to the bakery

Jean-Michel Wilmotte 1994

Baixa to Chiado

Jean-Michel Wilmotte 1994

on the east side and a dilapidated pavilion on the west, and it was Wilmotte's task to link these disparate parts. Accordingly, from the central hall, visitors are led on an upward journey through the labyrinthine galleries whose circuit follows that of the former museum rooms. A restrained, modernist palette of steel, stone and glass, white and greys, extends throughout and also recovers something of the spirit of the former convent. Dark timber porticoes create divisions between the various galleries and are used for window surrounds and furniture elements. Views between levels and galleries and an occasional glazed section of floor also reinforce the link between the elements. The materials used add to the calm and tranquillity that pervades the interior and which provides a cool oasis amid the colour, chaos and construction of the surrounding areas.

There are occasional glimpses of a seemingly unobtainable garden, which is eventually revealed at the end of the circuit. The haven of greenery rising above street level and trapped in the substantial external walls is a memory of the enclosed convent garden and looks over the city and the Tagus river.

Baixa to Chiado

ADDRESS Rua Serpa Pinto 6 [1N]
CLIENT Departamento da Cultura
TRAM 28 to Rua Victor Cordon
ACCESS Tuesday–Sunday 10.00–18.00

Jean-Michel Wilmotte 1994

Jean-Michel Wilmotte 1994

Portuguese Architects Association

The AAP occupies what was once Sao Paulo's Baths, a Neoclassical building belonging to the 'Companhia de Águas Medicinais do Arsenal de Lisboa' and used for medicinal purposes. The building was constructed in 1868 by Pedro J Pezerat; in the 1970s it was considered a relic of the city's industrial past and was saved from destruction by being made a listed building. Dressed in stucco with a portico and pediment, inside its main feature was an iron gallery overlooking the pool lit by an ornate skylight. Today only the building's façade and boundaries have been preserved.

In the early 1990s the building was offered to the AAP, which launched a competition to design its new headquarters in the baths. The renovation also marked an important step in the rehabilitation of this particular 'ribierinha' coastal zone, a rather tatty and rambunctious area still ranked by low life. The aim was to restore the building in a contemporary mode but one imbued with the history of the building, while adding a library, studies, and space for exhibitions and conferences.

The architects' response to the site and brief, and their expression of material and mass, seem wholly individual. The use of materials is playful, toying with the aesthetic by folding and tilting geometries which suggest an eccentric demeanour. Inside, the main impression given is informal and youthful, the space being open to natural light while individual spaces accommodate their own idiosyncrasies. A reception desk accosts the entrance hall with two, sharp, red-and-black projections from behind a bulky column enclosing the reception in its own bay, embodying the association's AA logo. Towards the middle of the building, and directly visible from the entrance, is the void that replaces the original baths. It has a spiralling series of balconies lit by the skylight which tops the building on the exterior and that act as a defunct viewing gallery. Brilliantly

Manuel Graça Dias and Egas José Vieira 1991–94

Baixa to Chiado

Manuel Graça Dias and Egas José Vieira 1991–94

coloured shards of broken ceramic tiles lining the cement wall on the ground floor bar are reminiscent of the old baths.

In all, materials and finishes have been used with great ingenuity and imagination and are boldly evocative of the association's image. This is carried through with conviction, especially in the display of normally bland and mundane standard ironmongery.

Baixa to Chiado

ADDRESS Travessa do Carvalho 21–5 [1M]
CLIENT AAP
TRAM 15, 17 from Praça do Commercio
to Rua de São Paulo
BUS 13, 60, 104 from Praça do Commercio
to Rua de São Paulo
ACCESS Monday–Friday 10.00–20.00,
Saturday 10.00–18.00

Manuel Graça Dias and Egas José Vieira 1991–94

Manuel Graça Dias and Egas José Vieira 1991–94

Restauradores to Parque Eduardo VII

Bimotor Records	58
Eden Aparthotel	60
Post Office	62
Victoria building	64
Tranquilidade Vida building	66
Heron Castillo building	68
Fashion Clinic	70
Rotunda I metro station	72
Rotunda II metro station	76
Anna Molinari shop	78
Parque Eduardo VII public lavatories	80
Coreto da Liberdade	82
Club VII	84

Bimotor Records

The building of the metro's new extension from the Restauradores to the Cais do Sodre (the train station linking Lisbon to its riviera) has affected the Baixa's main retailers. Bimotor Record's new glass box is a direct consequence of the owners' choice not to allow the building work to affect trade in what is a prime shopping locality. The temporary structure was erected a few metres from the original on the corner of this important square. It is no larger than the original shop and intentionally uses inexpensive materials to create an ephemeral design. The structure appears to be supported by a coloured boxed-metal beam that runs up, over and diagonally across the box, but in truth it only acts as a support for the bright red logo. A transparent glass façade surrounds the front of the structure, rendering it almost invisible except for the store's luminous logo. The back is left covered to avert attention from the construction-site hoarding.

This transient receptacle is an attempt to create a new image as well as providing a challenge to preconceived ideas about shopping in general – the concept is based on watching customers while they purchase goods. In many ways this sort of facility will affect a visitor's mind and spirit more than the permanent buildings around it.

It is perhaps surprising that this innovative structure was given planning permission, as it is surrounded by some of the more prestigious buildings on the Praça dos Restauradores.

ADDRESS Praça dos Restauradores 7 [2N]
COST £20,500
SIZE 3 x 6.5 square metres
METRO Restauradores
ACCESS open

Maria Fernanda Lamelas 1996

Maria Fernanda Lamelas 1996

Eden Aparthotel

The Eden was initially a 1930s theatre and cinema, but after it fell into decay it was extensively refurbished as an Aparthotel. However, as a listed building, the preservation of the interior staircase was believed to be of more importance in the modernist era than the preservation of the façade. Here, the new design combines a bold removal and perforation to the original façade creating behind it a semicircular curtain wall that houses the apartments and gives a view of the square. The staircase lobby is bright red with white handrails and stresses the striations so characteristic of the era. The lobby itself is overwhelming but it remains a vacant hall and acts as a restricted thoroughfare to the different parts of the Virgin Megastore housed over the ground floor and first-floor viewing galleries.

Restauradores to Parque Eduardo VII

ADDRESS Praça dos Restauradores [2N]
CLIENT Grupo Inogil
METRO Restauradores
ACCESS stairs and record store only;
10.00–22.00

Casino Branco 1937, G Pencreac'h and Frederico Valsassina 1996

Casino Branco 1937, G Pencreac'h and Frederico Valsassina 1996

Post Office

The Portuguese main post office commands an inspiring site on the Praça dos Restauradores in the centre of the city. The original building is characteristically Pombalino and was surrounded by a circulation ring with an internal courtyard that let light penetrate the interiors and was a space hidden from public view. The old services were performed through an awkward single door which led to a long and dark room with a stretched counter. The building was in desperate need of renewal and expansion to deal with the community at large and the many tourists.

The remodification has reinvigorated this large building with a series of subtle but weak interventions. Initially, the building's doors are opened to the square, creating a transitional hallway through several doorways. Subsequently, the organisation is such that the main functions are carried out in the covered courtyard immediately in front on the hall. An open, placid and airy space, painted bright pink, is tentatively adorned with oversized steel trusses. Tilting glass sections set in window cavities behind the counters obscure the view to the administrative offices. The counters' layout is slightly askew from the uniformity of the courtyard, leading and directing the visitor to the other facilities in an adjacent room and therefore creating a different exiting route with a fastidious approach.

ADDRESS Praça dos Restauradores [2N]
ASSOCIATE ARCHITECT Luis Miguel Pinto Rocha
CONTRACT VALUE £700,000 ·
SIZE 2000 square metres
METRO Restauradores
ACCESS open

Eduardo Lima Soares 1995

Restauradores to Parque Eduardo VII

Eduardo Lima Soares 1995

Victoria building

Lisbon is an old and reasonably small city condensed towards the river. One of the major problems facing most of its inner city developments, regardless whether they are business or residential, is the need for parking space. In the early 1970s, the government stipulated that buildings erected within the city boundaries would have to provide parking for tenants. Often designers choose to circumvent the problem by creating underground garages, but although the solution seems the easiest it contributes little at street level and interferes with pedestrian flow on the pavements. This is not the case in the Victoria building where the entrance is placed discreetly at the rear, allowing an elegant canopy at street level to shade pedestrians and giving an uninterrupted view of the shops. Insistent symmetry is more than made up for by the layers of fine steelwork in the windows, balconies, and the thorough and elegant detailing unusual to Lisbon.

ADDRESS Avenida da Liberdade 200 [4N]
METRO Avenida
BUS 1, 2, 9, 11, 21, 31, 32, 36, 39, 41, 44–46, 90
ACCESS shops only

Coelho da Silva Pinhiero 1997

Coelho da Silva Pinhiero 1997

Tranquilidade Vida building

Avenida da Liberdade is a lengthy, broad and picturesque tree-lined street intended for strolling. It is adorned either side with elegantly executed apartment buildings of the 1920s and 1930s, and with a number of amenities close by. Nevertheless, the buildings are being demolished and the street redeveloped as offices.

The Tranquilidade Vida building has a doubtful authenticity in its refinement, displacing an interpretation of mock 1930s connotations with glitzy modern materials which conceal its private function as well as trying to place the building in its context. The mask is distinguished by cross-bracing divided by an ornamental green granite plane canting above and over the roof, and ending abruptly just above street level with a stumpy sculpture of perforated steel which could be read as a dragon's face or body. This leads to a blunt and awkward entrance set off by two columns.

ADDRESS Avenida da Liberdade 230 [3M]
CLIENT Tranquilidade Vida, SA
SCULPTOR José Aurelio
METRO Avenida
ACCESS none, visible from the street

Carlos Guedes de Amorin 1997

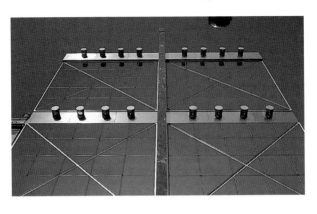

Restauradores to Parque Eduardo VII

Carlos Guedes de Amorin 1997

Heron Castillo building

The Avenida da Liberdade and its tributaries are distinguished by a mix of art-deco and art-nouveau heritage. It is rapidly being transformed: old buildings of architectural value are being redeveloped to alleviate the results of harsh modern construction. The Heron Castillo building, a modern office and residential block, falls into this category.

Currently, there are legal provisions for the conservation of old buildings enclosed within the city boundaries, often the only prerequisite being the preservation of façades to maintain the character of the street. The building's façade, now preserved, emphasises an exuberance of self-confidence and elegance typical of architecture of the turn of the century, but it is now stuck on a huge office block clad in a dark glass blandly detailed which serves only to intensify its banality.

ADDRESS Rua Braamcamp 40 [4M]
METRO Rotunda II
BUS 20, 22, 27, 38, 49
ACCESS none, visible from the street

Henrique Chicó 1992

Henrique Chicó 1992

Fashion Clinic

The area around the Avenida da Liberdade is busy with traffic flowing in and around the Praça do Marques Pombal, a major link with the bridge and other main routes to the commercial centre downtown. The Fashion Clinic introduces a new aspect to shopping interiors by establishing a dual function. The shop overlooks the street and its enclosed bar can be seen through its transparent façade, which enhances the airy and luminous interior, luring customers to the premises who can either stop for a drink, shop or do both. The temptation to shop is even greater at dusk and on wet days when light floods out to the street.

Finishes are delicate and handsome throughout the store and provide a backdrop for the clothes. The scheme uses a remarkable number of pure geometric forms heightened with light and natural materials, and all possessing a kind of light-filled simplicity and grace. The effect is a time-less elegance that contrasts with the bustling street outside and gives a refuge to shoppers or those just wanting a coffee.

ADDRESS Avenida da Liberdade 249 [4M]
METRO Rotunda II
ACCESS 10.00–18.00

Rashid Din 1996

Restauradores to Parque Eduardo VII

Rashid Din 1996

Rotunda I metro station

The city is renovating, remodelling and extending its metro lines and stations, and at the same time creating others to reach Expo 98, the city's periphery and the Cais do Sodre railway station on the river front. Rotunda I was built as part of an initial single line in the first phase of the metro's construction in the late 1950s. It has only been in the past 10 years that extensive refurbishment and additional stations have been added to the network (for example, page 76). Until now most of the stations have been designed as simple, long and linear voids often embellished in traditional tiles, painted and decorated by local artists. Rotunda I represents a prototypical example of the new modifications. Infused with sculptural form and designed to link the shopping zone directly below ground with the platforms, the architects have grasped the opportunity to create a public domain. An oval-shaped hall intersected by a central row of concrete columns forms the main arrival and exit area from the trains. Beyond, the ticket booth is a distinctively unhindered abstraction that defies rigorous definition: it is effectively a superimposition of a simple linear space by extrusions and overlapping planes on the walls and ceilings with the occasionally wedge-shaped surface disintegrating into an upright wall.

The station is an interchange with the city's only other line, served by Rotunda II (see page 76). Both stations are interlocked by a sweeping curve of shops on the outside (though they are still underground) and by a large interconnecting hall lit by the entrance stairwells. The Avenida da Liberdade entrance above ground has an unusual and sculptural-looking object this is in fact a lift, especially for the disabled. It is often out of order and is regularly polluted and used as a urinal because of its position, situated away from the vigilant eyes of the police (there is a police station directly below the entrance to the lift). Rotunda I is distin-

João Santa-Rita and José Santa-Rita 1992–95

Restauradores to Parque Eduardo VII

João Santa-Rita and José Santa-Rita 1992–95

guished by the green tones and labyrinthine vitality in its vaults and tilted walls which cant gradually to conceal the structure. Unfortunately, it is difficult to appreciate the station's design as its low claustrophobic ceiling hinders views of the magnificent structure.

Restauradores to Parque Eduardo VII

ADDRESS Praça do Marques Pombal [4M]
CLIENT Metropolitano de Lisboa, EP
METRO Rotunda I
ACCESS open

João Santa-Rita and José Santa-Rita 1992–95

Restauradores to Parque Eduardo VII

João Santa-Rita and José Santa-Rita 1992–95

Rotunda II metro station

Rotunda II metro station is part of the future sunflower line, which presently terminates here but will eventually connect further east with the Rato quadrant.

Symmetry plays an important part to this interchange, in comparison with its counterpart, Rotunda I (page 72), which is merely a jumbled network of planes. Neither of the two spaces are the same, although they are linked thematically by two channels and by the stone detailing on either entrance.

The space is large and airy and is easily comprehensible with tall, rectangular columns ascending to a never-ending gridded ceiling in a double-height void, which is interrupted by a rectangular mezzanine.

A prelude to the Marques de Pombal roundabout, this symmetrical deck is open, friendly and inviting, is unhindered by ticket gates and has a piazza-like appearance.

ADDRESS Praça do Marques Pombal [4M]
CLIENT Metropolitano de Lisboa, EP
METRO Rotunda II
ACCESS open

Duarte and Nuno Simões 1995

Restauradores to Parque Eduardo VII

Restauradores to Parque Eduardo VII

Duarte and Nuno Simões 1995

Anna Molinari shop

The latest Anna Molinari women's fashion shop occupies a prominent position on the south side of Rua Joaquim Antonio Aguiar, facing the Ritz Hotel and the Parque Eduardo VII. The street, however, is seen as a hazardous boundary between the two sides. The uncommitted and modest exterior yields little of what is going on inside, other than for the elegant set of door handles, which today are slightly vandalised, and it is easy to walk past or mistake the shop for another lifeless version.

The interior is an elegant, modelled space designed exclusively for the exhibition of the latest fashions. Materials and finishes have been used with great ingenuity, imagination and a delicate touch. The walls have an off white, almost grey colour and are occasionally wrapped in additional stainless steel sheets to give them a sharp, crisp and almost sterile quality which is washed away by the presence of an occasional etched rose. This is echoed by a red rose set in a black mosaic insert surrounded by a concrete floor.

ADDRESS Rua Joaquim Antonio Aguiar 35 [4M]
CLIENT Vicente & Ranito, LDA
METRO Rotunda 1
ACCESS open

Shay Peri 1997

Restauradores to Parque Eduardo VII

Shay Peri 1997

Parque Eduardo VII public lavatories

The Parque Eduardo VII has been reinvigorated by this elegant and self-confident public lavatory. The poetic quotations adhered to this unique little building seem apt for what could have been a dull and banal structure.

Essentially, the building is made of two components: a tapering, external mauve wall that rises gradually from the entrance to form a helical core and a large, orthogonal stone wall that bisects it. The juxtaposition of the two geometries gives added interest, creating an internal division between the male and female facilities which are announced by large flamboyant figures at the doors. The interior walls are decorated with blue glazed mosaics that add coolness and provide temporary relief from the Mediterranean heat. Daylight penetrates the structure through floor-to-ceiling-height glazing, and along a gap created by the spiral tapering between the internal and external walls, in turn deliberately forming a strip for plants.

This building is a strong attempt but a small gesture by the city's council to better the city's park and its life.

ADDRESS Parque Eduardo VII, in front of Praça do Marques Pombal [4M]
CLIENT Camãra Municipal de Lisboa (CML)
METRO Rotunda I or II
ACCESS open

Joaquim Quimarães 1997

Restauradores to Parque Eduardo VII

Joaquim Quimarães 1997

Coreto da Liberdade

Resembling more of an unidentified flying object than its true function, the Coreto is simply a bandstand. It is constructed with a cylindrical concrete block dressed in stone and partially buried in a brick floor. Its circular covering with a wooden underlay is held by three steel posts sheathed in copper. The disc's chief function is to provide a kinetic shelter that can move up and down as well as tilting back and forth, allowing the Coreto to adapt to multiple functions. It is surrounded by a mini amphitheatre and cadenced foliage.

Restauradores to Parque Eduardo VII

ADDRESS Parque Eduardo VII, beside the Carlos Lopes Pavilion [5M]
CLIENT Departamento de Desporto
METRO Parque
ACCESS open

Carlos Roque 1996–97

Carlos Roque 1996–97

Club VII

To reach Club VII, enter Parque Eduardo VII from its top end (off Avenida Cardeal Cerejeira) and walk down its right-hand side – note the views of the Tagus river – until the canopies of the tennis courts appear. Although the club was built on a green site, it created a facility that amalgamated the numerous sports facilities previously only found on the outskirts of the city.

The building is an incongruous box with elevations coarsely mottled with brick and concrete. It reflects an approach to detailing that is expressively robust, expressing the concrete structural frames. The composition is detached from the tall, undulating canopy of the sheltered tennis courts.

ADDRESS Parque Eduardo VII, beside the Rua Castilho [5M]
METRO Rotunda 1
ACCESS open

João Vasconcelos and Carlos Marques 1997

João Vasconcelos and Carlos Marques 1997

Amoreiras to Campolide

Amoreiras complex 88
Edificio Alto das Amoreiras 92
Arpad Szenes–Vieira da Silva Foundation 94
Patio da Bagatella 98
Universidade Nova, canteen and dormitory 102

Amoreiras complex

Less then a decade after the 1974 revolution, Lisbon witnessed the arrival of immigrants from its now-independent colonies. With few amenities to cater for this rise in the population, the city built the Amoreiras complex. The complex is an important Tomás Taveira work and demonstrates just how potent and popular the eclecticism of twentieth-century architecture can be. Abundant with pop and classical references, and with an innovative colour scheme, the complex is a polemic vision of architecture seen through colour, decoration and urban grandeur, a statement never seen in Lisbon and one that gave rise to a new master architect. In political terms architecture was no longer seen as a direct response to the social and political characteristics of the dictatorial age and was seen instead as a lively and approachable idiom of a new age.

The complex appears as a citadel dominating the city's highest point. It has acquired fame for being Lisbon's centre, but it overlooks and is adjacent to one of the more rundown areas, recognised as Lisbon's own Skid Row. The complex is ostentatious and consists of three mirrored office towers (each with its own individual crown and occupying about 20,000 square metres), with an ensemble of 115 luxury apartments, a shopping centre of 240 shops, 52 restaurants, ten cinemas and underground parking for 1200 vehicles.

A coloured arcade stretches along the periphery of the complex. Slightly removed from the building, it guides the visitor to an entry point. The interior is confusing with an agglomeration of oversized and obtrusive columns that dazzle the eye and shadow the shops. The eccentric colour palette adds to the confusion and does not facilitate its directional route. Taveira has adopted the curious practice of assigning function to his sculptural objects. For example, a fountain in the form of a whimsical composition is situated below the atrium at the heart of the centre and

Tomás Taveira 1980–87

rises from a pool and cuts through the first floor. Placed behind the stairs it forces users either side of it. It is, nevertheless, a clever device to distract and confuse the eye from the unfortunate emptiness below the stairs. Free-standing structures are scattered throughout the centre, one being the cinema's box office. However, the cinemas themselves are hopelessly scattered throughout the complex and are difficult to find.

Today the paint work is fading and a lack of cleaning provisions and facilities has made the building a bit tawdry, but the centre is still proving popular with both locals and visitors alike.

ADDRESS Avenida Eng. Duarte Pacheco [4K]
SIZE 58,000 square metres total area
BUS 11, 15, 23, 48, 53, 58
ACCESS shopping centre only

Tomás Taveira 1980–87

Tomás Taveira 1980–87

Edificio Alto das Amoreiras

The building is simply an office conglomeration dwarfed by the much larger complex of the Amoreiras (see page 88). Between them is a reservoir and road junction, which means that the open space gives the building a view from its prettiest side. The structure backs on to what is one of the city's run-down districts.

With an obvious consideration for its site, the building's façade is dressed in several layers that appear to undergo a transfiguration. The governing mirrored façade, which is smooth and curved at one end, reflects its surroundings in fragments; the other end is intercepted by a concrete grid, detaching itself from the interior and exposing its structural elements, and abruptly ending at the point above its meagre entrance. This in turn is attacked by and attached to a dispersed red steel frame.

The rear, south-facing wall disdainfully exposes its concrete cladding. It is overpowered by rows of windows and is shadowed by overhanging louvres that seemingly sneer at the building's neighbours.

Amoreiras to Campolide

ADDRESS Rua J Gomes Ferreira 4, a continuation of Rua D João V [4K]
BUS 15 from Cais do Sodre, 58 from Praça do Principe Real
ACCESS none, visible from the street

Rodrigues Fernandes 1995

Rodrigues Fernandes 1995

Arpad Szenes–Vieira da Silva Foundation

The initial objectives of the foundation were to promote and divulge an awareness and appropriate a study for the work of both Arpad Szenes and Vieira da Silva. The latter was frequently offered commissions by the metro company and a large number of her ceramic works may be seen cladding stations – especially older ones – throughout Lisbon.

Essentially, the building is a museum set in the boundaries of a redundant silk factory, the project being appropriately contemporary and unmistakably of its place. Although the design does not reflect the lucid and distinctive connection between this husband-and-wife team, it does, however, express the wishes of the late da Silva which were to reflect on the building's history and to refer to the serenity and austerity of the original eighteenth-century building by the Marques de Pombal and its site. The latter was chosen on the grounds that both the artists lived in the vicinity.

Overlooking Praça das Amoreiras, the outside of the building is draped in a distinctive Pombalino yellow, and other than a modest sign there is little to indicate the existence of a foundation or museum. The building is generated from a palette of marble, plaster and light-coloured wood. The floors are all of marble, as is the reception desk other than for a friendly wooden counter that appears to float above. The visitor's route through the internalised galleries is marked by a limpid wash of light. A tranquil spot for contemplation is created above a few steps between the entrance hall and the main exhibition gallery; this acts as a transition point. The main gallery is noteworthy for its A-frame-trussed roof structure that characterises the pitched ceiling. Although typical of the building's historical origins, the roof is altogether a rare sight in modern Portuguese construction as wood is expensive and requires skilled labour

José Sommer Ribeiro 1990

Amoreiras to Campolide

José Sommer Ribeiro 1990

to handle it.

The silence, grace and spaciousness of the building are almost equal to those of the square fronting the entrance, providing an almost meditative enviroment.

Amoreiras to Campolide

ADDRESS Praça das Amoreiras 58 [4L]
CLIENT Camãra Municipal de Lisboa (CML)
BUS 15 from Cais do Sodre to Rato, then walk up Rua Amoreiras
METRO Rato
ACCESS Wednesday–Monday 12.00–20.00, fee; free entry Monday

José Sommer Ribeiro 1990

José Sommer Ribeiro 1990

Amoreiras to Campolide

Patio da Bagatella

Patio da Bagatella is a picturesque site evoking memorable images of harmony and reinterpreting the traditional in a modern setting. It is a mixture of new build with the remodelling of the old factory's houses that formed part of life in the late eighteenth century, and which overlook the development's main asset, its courtyard.

These buildings are best described as a quadrangle sustaining a level of the secret and unexpected. The building is neither grim nor uninviting – it is hardly seen from the street because it is inward-looking, intimate and self-contained. The most formal entrance (on Rua San Filipe Nery) is through an axial opening, leading the visitor to the uppermost and covered forecourt (off axis) where local workers enjoy their lunch. Visitors are encouraged further into the space by a concrete trough of running water which leads down a few steps and into a small pool decorated with sculptures, a setting for substantial public-art initiatives. Here the quadrangle opens up to provide views for shop-keepers, office workers and residents.

The building's upper levels are south facing, making the most of the daylight. The height of the courtyard is articulated by tall concrete columns which lead the eye up to the sky and clearly endow the building with a sense of place. Shops on the first floor are sheltered by a walkway covered in creeper-clad, pergola-like trusses. The concrete is invariably load-bearing and has pink *ajuleijos* (tiles) for cladding with dark green for the other trimmings.

The Patio da Bagatella is architecture with a moral purpose and based on a perception of context, history and local culture. The development manages to establish a distinct environment of a bustling communal space, one that sets out to civilise its users. The scheme is obviously designed as place-making rather than as an object building. In fact its exte-

J M D Ferreira and M A Souza 1994–96

J M D Ferreira and M A Souza 1994–96

rior spaces and materials are clearly distinguishable from the bland interiors of the stores.

ADDRESS Patio da Bagatella,
Rua Artilharia 1-51 [4L]
CLIENT Jardim Bagatella
BUS 11, 23, 48, 53
to Rua Joaquim Ant Aguiar
ACCESS open

J M D Ferreira and M A Souza 1994–96

J M D Ferreira and M A Souza 1994–96

Universidade Nova, canteen and dormitory

The Universidade Nova occupies a site on a hillside in a previously unfashionable district. This dreary north-western corner of the city overlooks the Parque Monsanto. The area has been renamed Nova Campolide to differentiate it from the already existing crude and run-down residential Campolide and to provide an incentive which forms part of a rejuvenation plan to encourage new development and luxury apartments. More specifically, development of this languishing zone extends the boundary of city.

The roughly rectangular site is parallel to the Avenida Caloste Gulbenkian, a major route linking the Praca de Espanha to the 25 de Abril bridge and the IC15, the motorway which heads west. The site's hillside position overlooks the elegant mid-eighteenth-century aqueduct, one of the few remaining examples of John V's reign. Despite its adjacency to the Faculty of Economics, the building is secluded from the rest of the departments and the city centre, in what may almost be recognised as asuburb.

A new addition to the university, which houses both dormitories and a canteen, has a distinctively modern and instructive geometry. The new architecture holds itself back in respect to the old. A single, large white block seems to rise from the sandwiching of rectangular planes. This is truncated at either end by a series of steel-louvred, rectilinear cages that protect the stairs. Its linearity is interrupted by an additional protruding stairwell situated at the heart of the composition. This is further delineated along the smooth skin surface at the rear where several horizontal slits running down the its height denounce the stairs at these key points, contrasting with the vertical window grooves between. Its strictly solid and upright presence is visible from a distance as an abstract form rising

Manuel Tainha 1997

Amoreiras to Campolide

Manuel Tainha 1997

from the landscape. Although misleadingly dogmatic in appearance, the building is actually pragmatic by nature.

Amoreiras to Campolide

ADDRESS Travessa Estevão Pinto,
off Rua de Campolide [6L]
CONTRACT VALUE £2 million
BUS 15, 58 to Rua de Campolide
ACCESS grounds only

Manuel Tainha 1997

Manuel Tainha 1997

Alges, Belém and Santo Amaro

Alges bus station 108
Belém cultural centre 112
School of Architecture, Technical University of Lisbon (UTL) 116
Doca do Santo bar 118
Café da Ponte 120
Doca Louca, news kiosk and bar 124
Santo Condestável apartments 126

Alges bus station

Alges bus station is a superb marker of place, with its own unique, identifiable image. It avoids the usual problems associated with bus stops and stations, which end up being ubiquitous and anonymous, and provide no clues to their location. Its location is at the heart of an intersection, the gate to Alges. Links by road into Lisbon and the Estoril riviera begin and end here and the railway is within a stone's throw – an ideal site for a bus station.

The aim was to rationalise this traffic system by grouping a variety of facilities for the traveller, giving easy access to other public facilities, in what is ultimately the last stop to the west of the city centre.

The bustling station itself is neither a building nor a terminus in which to house buses. It is a simple structure used primarily for the sale of tickets but it does have other facilities for the traveller. Located at the end of a row of buildings, it overlooks a large, open square with bus shelters of granite and glass that provide little shade from the afternoon sun, a failure in the design concept. Customers hide behind instead of under the shelters, as their mass provides better protection.

The main structure is centred around a tall granite tower with two large planes that appear to float above and shield its components. The taller of these planes hovers, curves and cants towards the lower one, providing a shelter for the open terraced roof of the café and the shop below. The planes, although curved in plan, are supported by a string of slender columns which run elegantly along the length of the front of the building.

With a mainly glazed façade, the bus station appears to be divided into three distinct sections: the café (the larger of the divisions), the ticket office (overlapped on top by the café) and a final section with a newsagent and shops. The dark granite cladding merges well with the now pedes-

Carlos Marques 1994

Alges, Belém and Santo Amaro

Carlos Marques 1994

trianised square beside it. The square is a gratifying pedestrian walkway leading to Alges and is conspicuous because of its linear but scattered pattern of tree saplings, white figurines and an array of seats, providing a gentle and relaxing gateway into the city.

ADDRESS Praça D Manuel [12D]
TRAIN from Cais do Sodre to Alges
TRAM 15
BUS 23 from Praça do Marques Pombal
ACCESS open

Carlos Marques 1994

Alges, Belém and Santo Amaro

Carlos Marques 1994

Belém cultural centre

Belém cultural centre is situated in a region with some of Portugal's most important heritage buildings, such as the sixteenth-century Mosteiro dos Jeronimos. This historical site overlooking the Tagus river is a bold symbol of Lisbon's architectural, economic and political renewal. Portugal officially joined the European Union in 1992, and set about commissioning a competition-winning design from Vittorio Gregotti to house the European Commission, the presidency of which is held by each member state for 6 months in rotation. Portugal's presidency was in 1997.

The origins of the centre's urban framework lie in the urban design policy of the New State when in 1938 it staged 'The Portuguese World Exhibition' to exalt the country's nationalism. The modern building is constructed on the same site and is now the largest cultural edifice built since 1974 since the downfall of the Salazar's dictatorial rule. The centre is multifunctional and forms an integral part of the square, as seen particularly from the Tagus, and its contextual sensibilities appear to compete with the surrounding heritage simply due to its mass. However, the bulk is dissolved by the centre's horizontality along and above the railway line, the stepping down away from the square, and the cutting through of its mass to disclose an apparent open core. Where the scheme faces the Praça do Imperio a perforation made to the fascia creates an opening below the main administrative building which leads to a quadrangle surrounded by shops and shaded by the surrounding building towering above. Another bright, open and friendly quadrangle is revealed eventually after a linear journey via ramps and stairs.

As a whole the building is perceived as a huge citadel with indentations and a slightly incongruous roofline. In fact, it is segmented into two divisions, administrative and cultural, and is preceded physically by a hierarchy of height, with a sloped incision dividing the two and bearing a

Alges, Belém and Santo Amaro

Vittorio Gregotti 1988–93

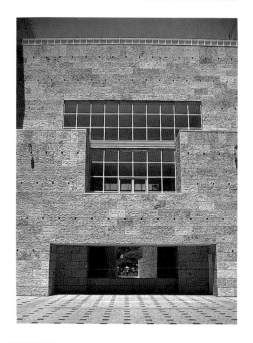

Alges, Belém and Santo Amaro

Vittorio Gregotti 1988–93

series of ramps and stairs interconnecting different zones and levels. From the quadrangles recessed bays reveal uninterrupted views of the river and Maritime Museum.

The centre is faced with rough limestone offset by the white, detailed frames around entrances and windows. Transparent walls disclose the interiors which open mainly on to the inner courtyards. The interior is a subtle but rigorous scheme that expresses a relationship with the exterior. This is apparent especially in the whitewashed exhibition rooms that reflect and disclose a series of long corridors interconnected by ramps in zenith-like spaces and, occasionally, revealing a hidden exterior courtyard or gardens. The forms and materials of the whole appear to respect the building's context while presenting an excellent and diaphanous public front. However, the good work is overshadowed by the centre's extreme mass.

A further and final addition to the centre has been planned, with a square dominated by a hotel, leading to a new street of shops and housing. This final stage is yet to be realised as funds were diverted to build Expo.

ADDRESS Praça do Imperio [1B]
ASSOCIATE ARCHITECT RISCO – Manuel Salgado
STRUCTURAL ENGINEERS STA Segadaes Tavares Associados, LDA
INTERIOR Daciano Costa
TRAIN from Cais do Sodre to Belém
TRAM 15
ACCESS open

Vittorio Gregotti 1988–93

Vittorio Gregotti 1988–93

School of Architecture, Technical University of Lisbon (UTL)

The School of Architecture occupies an enviable site on a hill in the Parque Florestal de Monsanto and has magnificent views of the Tagus river. The design represents a new concept for the school: previously it was scattered throughout the city centre but now is all on one site, rather like a small city in itself.

The structure's base consists of a tall, central core surrounded by open spaces and three long rows, two containing classrooms while the other has the social services areas. Classrooms are set side by side and each has a workshop on a mezzanine that is screened from the room by a simple, retractable partition. While expressing a rational design, the all-white school is aesthetically harmonious but can be subdued at times, and is often considered too bland an environment for the creative impulses of its students.

Alges, Belém and Santo Amaro

ADDRESS Alto da Ajuda [4F]
CLIENT Gabinete das Novas Instalacoes for Universidade Tecnica de Lisboa
BUS 23 from Praça do Marques Pombal (recommended), 42 from Avenida Duque Dávila (lengthy route)
ACCESS grounds only

Augusto Brandão 1994

Alges, Belém and Santo Amaro

Augusto Brandão 1994

Doca do Santo bar

A relic of Lisbon's industrial past, this dock has been remodelled to engage with the busy commercial life of the city. The abandoned and dilapidated warehouses fronting the marina became part of the socialist government's plans to extricate and relocate the bars and night life of the Bairro Alto in the city centre, an area considered unsuitable because of its old and small residential high quarter. The plan has not worked well because most of the bars are new, none having moved here from the old quarter. Doca do Santo is one of the first bars to take advantage of this regeneration and occupies an autonomous unit that differentiates it from the rest of the prosaic development.

During the day the bar spills out into its glass box, so a visitor will never truly appreciate the interior elements which are constructed from industrial materials reminiscent of the old docks. The main building is used mainly at night and is more atmospheric. Its best feature is a staircase set at an angle in the wall, almost as if a crate has crashed through it. A dividing glass strip allows views through this stair block, and is best seen from the motorway to the north.

ADDRESS Doca de Santo Amaro [1G]
SIZE 390 square metres
TRAIN Cais Sodre to Alcantara Mar (not to be confused with Alcantara Terra)
TRAM 15 to Alcantara
BUS 28, 32 to Alcantara
ACCESS open

Arquitectos, LDA 1994–96

Alges, Belém and Santo Amaro

Arquitectos, LDA 1994–96

Café da Ponte

Neon lights flash across the rippling water. The clatter of crockery and the bustle of people now permeate an area that has witnessed the decline of shipbuilding and manufacturing, leaving a large tract of dereliction. In 1994 a strategic plan was drawn up with the aim of revitalising the fragmented post-industrial zones close to the centre, catapulting the city into the next millennium.

Café da Ponte is sited on a promenade along a stretch of the harbour that has gradually developed into a modern cultural and commercial riverside strip, and is now the base for a small fishing fleet and some leisure craft.

The café is settled in a striking series of archetypal simple forms, each identifiable by its own symmetrical double-pitched roof, and is part of a development that has many kitsch and themed bars in the adjoining rejuvenated warehouses (see page 118). The promenade strip runs the length of the development from the elegant 1940s Alcantara Maritime Station to just under the 25 de Abril bridge, which marks the end of the dock. The café often hosts art exhibitions and book launches for the many visitors to the area.

The old pitched roof has been removed and replaced with a wing-like structure that forms an expressive lid to differentiate this independent-minded building from its less architecturally inspired neighbours. This creates a restaurant on the first floor above the café with magnificent views of the dramatic sweep of the river. Sustained by a floating slab of concrete detached from the glazed exterior walls, the roof allows daylight to flood the interior space below.

Like most other cafés in Lisbon, form and materials make up for the lack of details. The interior is cheerful with a mix of colours, from the wood lining the stairwell and the vertical toilet block, to the blue mosaic

Alges, Belém and Santo Amaro

Rui Orfáo 1995

Rui Orfão 1995

of the horizontal bar. The exterior façade consists of steel mullions and a frame supporting sliding doors that open the bar out on to the promenade.

Alges, Belém and Santo Amaro

ADDRESS Doca de Santo Amaro, warehouse 18 [1G]
CLIENT PRO-Profisional de Otilaria, LDA
TRAIN Cais Sodre to Alcantara Mar (not to be confused with Alcantara Terra) TRAM 15 to Alcantara BUS 28, 32 to Alcantara
ACCESS open

Rui Orfáo 1995

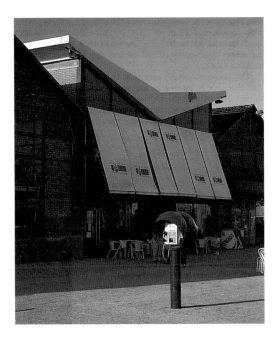

Algés, Belém and Santo Amaro

Rui Orfão 1995

Doca Louca, news kiosk and bar

The Doca Louca, news kiosk and bar is an integral part of the varied and busy commercial life of the docks and provides literary sustenance previously unavailable in the area. The structure is based around an idealistic paradigm of genuinely mixed use and as such is carefully inserted in the existing fabric.

This is contemporary architecture with neither right angles nor verticals that creates an elegant and jaunty sculptural form. Through clever cutting and jointing the architect has invested in traditionally robust and industrial materials to create a spectacular facility which, with angled roofs to protect the enclosed space from the sun, casts elaborate shadows throughout the day.

Algés, Belém and Santo Amaro

ADDRESS Doca de Santo Amaro [1G]
TRAIN Cais Sodre to Alcantara Mar
(not to be confused with Alcantara Terra)
TRAM 15 to Alcantara
BUS 28, 32 to Alcantara
ACCESS open

Arquitectos, LDA 1997

Alges, Belém and Santo Amaro

Arquitectos, LDA 1997

Santo Condestável apartments

The Santo Condestável apartment block has been decorated by wallpaper merchants (the current president of the Association of Architects). The building does little to enhance the surrounding neighbourhood with its mixture of pink and grey tiles. The interiors are dark and small, although they do offer excellent views of the Santo Condestável church and square.

Algés, Belém and Santo Amaro

ADDRESS Rua Azedo Gneco 82
– Campo de Ourique [3J]
TRAM 28
ACCESS none, visible from the street

Filipe Jorge Silva and Olga Quitanilha 1997

Alges, Belém and Santo Amaro

Filipe Jorge Silva and Olga Quitanilha 1997

Saldanha to Arieiro

31 de Janeiro market 130
Office at Avenida Duque de Avila, 185 134
Executive Inn Hotel 136
Bank National Ultramarino 138
Alif Hotel 142
Caixa Geral de Depositos 144
Stivali shoe shop 148

31 de Janeiro market

Originally the old market was sited at the corner of the Rua Eng. Vieira da Silva and Avenida Fontes Pereira Melo. It was somewhat dilapidated and had serious problems generally with the standard of hygiene and day-to-day running, especially the movement of produce. The site was strategically important for the development of an associated shopping complex and additional apartments which integrate with the existing development in Saldanha square. When the municipality was approached for the purchase of this essential corner site for the shopping complex and apartments they agreed to the purchase but only with the proviso that a new market be built to replace the old one.

The purpose-built structure is planned simply as a linear concrete shed, mimicking the unadorned functionalism of the market. The rectangular volume is set parallel to the street and is designed with an enduring simplicity and austere inclination. The interior spreads over three floors with two trading levels above ground, and parking and delivery areas below. A detached administrative section is extruded from the rest of the building adjacent to an entrance opposite the Rua Actor Taborda. This is set back slightly from the rest of the building and is emphasised by a dark brown-painted exterior that projects into the roof space, where there is a baseball pitch.

The main entrance – rarely used – is glazed, exposing a typically Portuguese restaurant which serves the local community as well as the market workers. The more commonly used side entrance has direct access to the first floor via a large staircase and by a long ramp along its monolithic wall. The ramp is used not only by the tenants to wheel their trolleys, but also by the public.

Inside, rows of trading posts – equally divided between meats above and fruit and vegetables below – are lined up along the centre. Lighting

João Paciência 1996

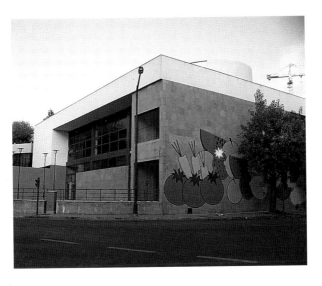

João Paciência 1996

Saldanha to Arieiro

is strictly fluorescent, while air is circulated mechanically and is expelled at ground-floor level on to Jose Fontana square – unfortunately for the passer-by who, unaware of the presence of a vent system, is liable to be overwhelmed by the stench of fish.

ADDRESS Rua Eng. Vieira da Silva [5N]
CLIENT Camãra Municipal de Lisboa (CML)
METRO Picoas
BUS 20, 22, 27 from Rotunda roundabout, 32 from Rossio
ACCESS 07.00–14.00

João Paciência 1996

Saldanha to Arieiro

João Paciência 1996

Office at Avenida Duque de Avila, 185

This office development is based in the Avenidas Novas (new avenues), an apparently residential area, often criticised because of its speculative urbanism and low cultural profile. The black façade is semantically fitting for a cool office space with a virtually flawless surface bulging out above street level and it allows no visual access from the street. Even the number of the building, although occupying a whole wall surface, is hidden from public gaze. The building curves around the site awkwardly, ending in a shard whose reflections fragment the environment, mitigating the development's rather sinister image.

ADDRESS Avenida Duque de Avila, 185 [6N]
CLIENT Imovator
SIZE 8538 square metres
METRO Saldanha
BUS 16, 18, 42
ACCESS none, visible from the street

Regino Cruz 1996

Saldanha to Arieiro

Regino Cruz 1996

Executive Inn Hotel

The 72-room hotel fronts the quasi-pedistrianised Avenida Conde Valbom, a quiet residential street on axis with the Calouste Gulbenkian Foundation Headquarters (which contains the Modern Arts Centre designed by Sir Leslie Martin *et al* and built in 1983). The street is part of a municipal programme which aims to enrich and refurbish some of the city's green and pedestrian spaces, to reduce parking on pavements, to increase pavement widths and to upgrade facilities such as lighting and fountains. As a prerequisite, new building projects are forced to include parking spaces, the result being underground facilities which have their entrances at street level, disrupting the flow of pedestrians and destroying all chances of a pavement culture.

The building is distinguished by a stone façade adorned with a gridded division of windows by steel rods which serve as perches. Two spiral icons placed above the doors, and in keeping with the grid, repeat themselves throughout the interior on fittings such as the carpets and bed-side lamps. The interior is kept simple and friendly with little decoration, but the reception area has a liquorice all-sorts appeal.

Saldanha to Arieiro

ADDRESS Avenida Conde Valbom 56–62 [6N]
CLIENT Style Hotels
METRO Saldanha
BUS 16, 18, 42
ACCESS open

Didier Lefor 1990

Bank National Ultramarino

The Bank National Ultramarino was built during a political era when private greed and indifference to public values comprised the only acceptable creed. This building is just an enormous office block with all the amenities necessary for the normal functioning of an established bank.

The structure displays an equivocal architectural language of awesome proportions, especially with its use of a bright colour palette. Tall, thin concrete towers, which rise above blocks of glazing and which resemble the flared form of a Portuguese *fado* guitar, seem to hold the composition together. In fact, the design was highly influenced by the Fatima church of the 1940s (situated across the street) in conjunction with the towers of the Praça dos Touros (the bull-fighting ring in Campo Pequeno) built before the turn of the century. There is also little doubt that seven centuries of Moorish presence in the Iberian peninsula left a strong impression on the Portuguese.

A large pediment on thin columns announces the entrance to both the public and the private sectors of the bank. The entrance is both obscured and humanised by a mass of plants. The building's exterior is highly decorated in bright colours which mingle with the pink and dark striations of the marble employed. A parade of two-tone marble columns forms a colonnade around the lower street level, providing both shelter and an alternative entrance to the bank. It also supports a mid-level block overflowing with plants on to the street below.

Inside the building, Taveira has fashioned interiors like stage-set designs. With an abysmal interior colour composition of mints, pinks, yellows, greens and streaked white marble, the bank has a surreal dimension that goes beyond the decorum normally associated with such a structure. Undulating and sinuous curves, characteristic of this architect's

Tomás Taveira 1983–89

Tomás Taveira 1983–89

language, heighten this whimsy to produce a restless interaction and creates a mood which is particularly impressive at night.

ADDRESS Avenida 5 de Outubro 175 [7N]
SIZE 66,000 square metres
METRO Campo Pequeno
BUS 1, 21, 32, 36, 44, 45, 56
ACCESS open

Tomás Taveira 1983–89

Tomás Taveira 1983–89

Alif Hotel

The Alif Hotel is a florid structure that amounts to little more than a futile shed. It is distinguished by its shady colours, small and numerous pitched roofs, and a large cubic protrusion that announces its weak, narrow entry point. The bland foyer is badly designed: note the steps that lead down into it and the free-standing column. The rooms are also a tad kitsch.

Saldanha to Arieiro

ADDRESS Campo Pequeno 51 [60]
CLIENT Grupo Alif Hoteis
METRO Campo Pequeno
ACCESS open

Carlos Tamm 1983–91

Saldanha to Arieiro

Carlos Tamm 1983–91

Caixa Geral de Depositos

This mammoth building is the state's flagship bank. At the competition stage it received much adverse criticism. Initially presumed to be an enterprise for cultural development, the bank ended as an urban design challenge that added up to little more than market-led opportunism, paranoia indulging in post-modern icons. The building was meant to house all its major departments, which were previously dispersed throughout the city, though with hindsight the fundamental reason for its construction can be seen to be a need to secure its own autonomy as a single unit.

The building occupies a site in the heart of the city next to the bullfighting ring on a previously disused ceramics factory. The site was chosen for its good links with distributor routes, the Campo Pequeno being served by the metro, the railway and motorways, heading both to the north and the west.

Off the Avenida Joao XXI is an over-sized, porch-like structure with a pyramidal roof. It is connected to the principal entrance by a bridge, which acts as a gateway and allows a splendid view of the garden. In the garden a remnant of a chimney providing associations with the site's past history and scale stands by the side of a pool or moat which meanders the length of the site. Access to the bank is through awkwardly placed, heavy, rectangular copper gates. A feeling of monstrosity and intimidation are apparent from the entrance and is caused not only by the structure's size, but is also accentuated by the number of columns on its façade, which are necessary for earthquake protection.

The interior is accessed through stainless-steel doors. The main atrium is splendidly decorated but is nothing more than a glorified light-well. There is also no usual reception area and a distinct lack of information to guide a visitor to the array of services on offer. These range from standard banking provisions to cultural activities such a library, a 700-

Arsénio Raposo Cordeiro 1985–93

Arsénio Raposo Cordeiro 1985–93

seat auditorium for concerts and conferences, and a gallery for temporary exhibitions on a lower level reached either via the main atrium or from the curved entrance on Rua Arco do Cego. Some of the competitors' models for the project are also displayed in the banking hall on the main level. From these it is obvious that the building is truly gigantic, consisting of 14 storeys, six of which are below ground.

The employees like the building because of its architectonic value, better interior ambience, optimum functioning between departments and security. However, it is a disappointing project for those residents who live nearby in the Bairro Arco do Cego, a 1930s housing quarter which is dwarfed by the bank's size and separated from it by an amphitheatre designed by the architect and offered to the city.

Saldanha to Arieiro

ADDRESS Avenida Joao XXI [60]
CLIENT Caixa Geral de Depositos
SIZE 38,000 square metres
METRO Campo Pequeno
BUS 1, 21, 31, 32, 36, 44, 45, 54, 56
ACCESS open

Arsénio Raposo Cordeiro 1985–93

Arsénio Raposo Cordeiro 1985–93

Stivali shoe shop

The Portuguese take style seriously, particularly where footwear is concerned. Accordingly, the conditions in which shoes are sold are particularly important and Stivali is just one of a number of companies to promote good architecture.

The shop's design and space are predetermined by the concrete structure of the 1940s' shell. The architect's approach is a simple execution of a few casts of shades on the ceiling between the concrete structural beams. The interior is arranged in two distinct zones: public and ceremonial. The former admits the customer, the latter being out of sight and entered along a brushed stainless-steel staircase. The threshold is defined by a green canvas held by a delicate steel frame. The upper space is hidden from public view and has an intimate formality where the more discerning customer is fitted with bespoke shoes.

In general the shop's finish has a delicate and comfortable touch, and the work of the architect is apparent throughout, from the door bell to the design of interior fittings such as the tables.

There are other Stivali shops by Safira Serpa on Praça Dr Francisco Sá Carneiro 15-A [6P] and Rua Castillo 71-C [4M].

ADDRESS Avenida Joao XXI 11-C [6P]
CLIENT Frank e Casal, LDA
METRO Arieiros
BUS 20, 22 from Praça do Marques Pombal, 35 from Cais Do Sodre
ACCESS open

Safira Serpa 1997

Safira Serpa 1997

Cidade Universitária

Santos Reis church extension 152
Torre do Tombo 154
Psychology and Education Sciences Faculty 156
Cidade Universitária metro entrance 158
Pharmacy Faculty library 160
Swimming pool 162
ISCTE library 164

Santos Reis church extension

The extension to the church of Santos Reis is a departure from Frederico Valsassina's usual style. Taking the site into account, he has hoisted the extension above and behind the old church and, amid its dull and commercial neighbours, it strikes a resonant note of liveliness, freedom and individuality. Recognised for its iconoclastic quality, the building's form is fractured and distorted, transforming and creating a lively court-yard below.

The exposed structural concrete beams and columns are often disjointed and positioned at variable angles. They do not link up with their counterparts but instead create divisions that form crosses and generate an irregular structural rhythm. The contorted geometries are accentuated with a coating of white and blue highlighting.

The entrance is at the corner and is expressed by a fractured wall above. To the left is a simple ramp connecting the new addition with the old building, and beside it are glazed stair towers that provide views of the interior.

ADDRESS Campo Grande (east side), just off south corner with Avenida do Brazil [9N]
CLIENT Patriaco
SIZE 640 square metres
METRO Entre Campos or Alvalade
BUS 1, 45, 83
ACCESS church open

Cidade Universitária

Frederico Valsassina 1997

Cidade Universitária

Frederico Valsassina 1997

Torre do Tombo

The Torre do Tombo houses the state's historical archives and was the result of a competition-winning scheme. Its name derives from a medieval tower of the Castelo Sao Jorge [20], which incidentally also served as an archive.

As a monolithic and monstrous concrete structure in a large and open site on the university campus, the Torre competes with the surrounding, neat architectural arrangements. It announces itself quite forcibly with a brutal and austere composition, while the gargoyles on its four masses hover above a feeble and sloping dark curtain wall. The work is not dissimilar to the architects' usual work (such as the Caixa Geral de Depositos).

ADDRESS Alameda da Universidade [9M]
METRO Cidade Universitária
BUS 31, 35, 38, 68
ACCESS Monday–Saturday 09.00–17.00

Arsénio Cardoso and António Ferreira 1990

Cidade Universitária

Arsénio Cardoso and António Ferreira 1990

Psychology and Education Sciences Faculty

Situated directly opposite the Torre de Tombo (see page 154), the university's Psychology and Education Sciences Faculty sits more comfortably along the Alameda (grove) than its counterpart. In combining traditional materials and courtyards the architect has created a modern, humanly scaled enclosure, integrating it skilfully in the surrounding natural and man-made setting. The building is planned around a courtyard, within which small individual developments arise, replacing its neglected surroundings with trees, shrubs and a pond. It produces a distinctive sense of public and private, openings and enclaves respectively. This intimate and private courtyard is finished in stucco and painted a light ochre.

The exterior is clad in a lightly coloured, indigenous stone occasionally interrupted by the red steel of balconies which protrude from the surface. On the Alameda side a smooth wall is faced with an array of square windows lined up neatly along its ground-floor level, broken only by the larger entrance which fits well into the composition. This building was awarded the Valmor Architecture Prize in 1993.

ADDRESS Alameda da Universidade [9M]
METRO Cidade Universitária
BUS 31, 35, 38, 68
ACCESS grounds only

Manuel Tainha 1991

Cidade Universitária

Cidade Universitária

Manuel Tainha 1991

Cidade Universitária metro entrance

The entrance to this metro station pays homage to the Parisian civilians who escaped aircraft attack during the Second World War by hiding in the metro. The project was a gift to the university from the Metropolitan Company, both institutions being tremendous patrons of the arts and architecture. The actual design is by Maria Helena Vieira da Silva, an artist often commissioned by the Metro who works in the traditional Portuguese medium of *azulejo* (decorated glazed tile).

The architect uses ambiguity and diversity to create a spatial structure that does not actually shelter the traveller but instead provides a reference or strategic point which unites the university campus. The design is arranged around traces of broken grids and colours, inducing an effect of suppression and displacement.

Cidade Universitária

ADDRESS Avenida Professor
Gamma Pinto [9M]
ARTIST Maria Helena Vieira da Silva
METRO Cidade Universitária
ACCESS open

Manuel Cargalheiro 1989

Manuel Cargalheiro 1989

Pharmacy Faculty library

Until recently the library of the Pharmacy Faculty stood as a single, octagonal unit. The exterior is simply a shell clad, mostly in light blue mosaic and an array of slender, concrete, vertical fins that screen out the sun's rays. The main interior consists of a three-storey reading room around an empty volume which is lit from the north and provides a comfortable space in which to read. The room is contained by three slender columns that hold its tiered ceiling, and by a staircase cantilevered from an *in-situ* base in the void that leads up to the top gallery. Rooflights flood the interior void with more light which reflects off the walls to filter down into the reading spaces below.

The main reading area is in a recessed level, making the interior appear higher than the building seems from the outside. The books are stored on wooden shelving placed around the boundary walls, lessening the need for additional furniture. They are also held on the stair wall, which overlaps into the space and completely encloses the area with books.

Materials and finishes are delicate, with whitewashed walls situated between the exposed, structural grey concrete and the warmth of the wood used for the shelving, not unlike the ISCTE Library (see page 164).

The building no longer stands alone. Two years after its completion, was attached to a new and much larger building by a glazed bridge clad in the same exterior material.

ADDRESS Avenida Professor Gamma Pinto [8M]
CLIENT Ministro de Saúde, Universidade de Lisboa
CONTRACT VALUE new building £3 million
METRO Cidade Universitária
BUS 30–32, 55, 68
ACCESS grounds only

Raúl Hestnes Ferreira 1991–97

Raúl Hestnes Ferreira 1991–97

Swimming pool

The summer of 1997 saw the opening of the first Olympic-sized swimming pool in the heart of Lisbon. The complex is at the end of the linear Avenida Professor Gamma Pinto and is situated in the university grounds. The building is announced by a gate and a towering, large, cubic clock held up by two, thin concrete arms.

The complex has two covered and heated pools, one 50 by 25 metres, the other half its size. A VIP stand and a gym are housed under the span of the main pool, while restaurants, a bar, saunas and a first-aid centre are in the rest of the complex.

The main entrance is through a large glass block adjacent to an agglomeration of curved subsidiary brick walls and terraces. Swimmers enter the pool area through another linear and layered tube-like zone directly in front of the clock. This appears to support the primary structure, an elegant but bold span of steel fins encompassing the swimming pool. Between the soffits are strips of lights that illuminate the water.

ADDRESS Avenida Professor
Gamma Pinto [10M]
CLIENT Estádio Universitário de Lisboa
METRO Cidade Universitária
BUS 31, 35, 38, 68
ACCESS open

Frederico Valsassina 1997

Cidade Universitária

Frederico Valsassina 1997

ISCTE library

The ISCTE complex is a simple extension to the Institute of Management and Labour Sciences centre of documentation and is the first alteration to the original building since its completion 20 years ago. The extension sits like a building block on an old corner structure, but it is separated from the main structure due to environmental reasons and because it needed a formal identity, though its design is strongly conditioned by the adjacent, older building. The extension's angular geometry also fits in well with its surroundings. However separate the extension may appear, it is connected internally by ramps visible from the outside through large, rectangular windows.

The new wing is built of whitewashed concrete, the same material as its predecessor, but differences in the nature of their volumes reveal how the function of the Institute has changed over the past two decades.

The extension houses specialised books in a dedicated room away from the main library. They are stored in a double-height space with a mezzanine, reached via spiral stairs which are lit naturally by a small, circular skylight. Light has to be controlled and minimised in the extension to conserve the book collections.

The architect has managed to create an intimate and autonomous space for reading by keeping materials to a minimum (white-washed walls are mixed with grey, exposed, structural concrete), by designing the wooden furniture and by playing with natural light in a controlled manner.

ADDRESS Avenida Forças Armadas, backing on to the university campus [8N]
METRO Cidade Universitária or Entre Campos BUS 32, 55
ACCESS grounds only

Cidade Universitária

Raúl Hestnes Ferreira 1991–95

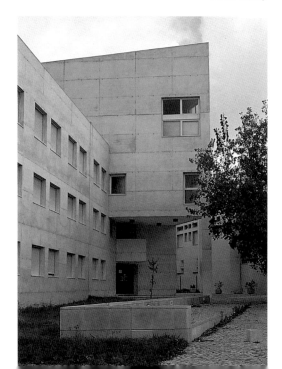

Benfica

BANIF bank 168
Lisboa Towers 170
St José Psychiatric Clinic 172
School Superior de Comunicaçao Social 174
Barrio do Bom Pastor 178
Colombo Centre 182

BANIF bank

Sete Rios is a district well known as the location of the city zoo. Recently, however, the creation of a major road network that links to the newly opened expressway to the 25 de Abril bridge has seen a steady growth in population and the rise of a small civic area.

The bank is easily identifiable along the linear Avenida José Malhoa, a wide street of office developments mixed with hotels and other buildings still under construction, because its oversailing aerofoil-like element forms a delicate yet expressive lid, or hat, over the green glass block below it. The building is outlined by another smaller building, and both are set back from pavement by a dignified and generous recess with a water spring that has no boundaries.

The larger building is defined mainly by glass that exposes steel works attached to an isolated concrete wall, whose side facing the building is clad in aluminium, its other side being blank.

The smaller building is a more public structure clad in dark granite and protected at arms length by a pewter grey aluminium wall. Like its larger neighbour, it too is surmounted by a lid, only this is punctured by a tree from the roof garden. The tree is a small poetic gesture that makes a considerable impact on the area's residents.

ADDRESS Avenida José Malhoa with Rua Delfim de Brito Guimarães [7K]
CLIENT BANIF
METRO Sete Rios
BUS 41 from Restauradores
ACCESS bank only

Benfica

Sua Kay 1995

Benfica

Sua Kay 1995

Lisboa Towers

Construction in the city centre is expanding quickly, but generally the main sites often have problematic planning requirements. Lisboa Towers takes a different tack, being situated on the green belt which forms the perimeter of the city. The periphery is generally urban with mediocre housing and commercial projects, but it is well connected to the major infrastructural projects of the moment.

Lisboa Towers is a major urban design project intended as a gateway for the new peripheral zone of Telheiras' intersection. It is well connected and has had a considerable impact on local business and the residential areas, by producing new resources and accommodating the nearby luxury housing communities with an up-market commercial centre.

The complex presently contains two towers, a third and a fourth are currently under construction. Their reflective coating gives a synthetic cleanliness that enriches the skyline around the east–west route of the Avenida General de Matos, a major link with the airport.

ADDRESS Rua A Albino Machado with Rua Tomás da Fonseca [10K]
CLIENT Grupo Inogi
SIZE 65,270 square metres total office, of which about 10 per cent is for commercial use
BUS nearest is off Estrada da Luz, then walk up Rua Lucio de Azevedo
ACCESS open

Benfica

Frederico Valsassina 1996–

Benfica

Frederico Valsassina 1996–

St José Psychiatric Clinic

Telheiras is a suburb that has recently had new developments and is already suffering from a lack of attention to the designed landscape, particularly the interaction between individual buildings. The psychiatric clinic was built before the city expanded into the area and it is now surrounded by luxury apartment blocks. As most of the area is still under construction with large private housing schemes (it is often referred to as Legoland), it is extremely difficult to evaluate its architecture, but early signs indicate that the suburb will have little context and no sense of community.

The clinic is at the heart of this chaotic and shambolic development. It sits in its own enclosed communal landscape which, fortunately, can be seen from the neighbouring towers and perhaps improves the life of ordinary citizens just a little.

The chapel, in particular, has an unusually shaped and striking, highly futuristic design that is a visual and social focus for the area and which attempts to bring some community spirit and civic pride to this peripheral district.

ADDRESS Quinta da Torre do Fato, Azinhaga da Torre do Fato [11K]
METRO Colégio Militar or Campo Grande
BUS 47, 67 to Rua Francisco Namora
ACCESS grounds and church only

Fernão L S de Carvalho and Cristina B S de Carvalho Blanc 1995

Benfica

Fernão L S de Carvalho and Cristina B S de Carvalho Blanc 1995

School Superior de Comunicaçao Social

It appears that recently the best hill sites around Lisbon have been given to public projects, the university campus being a good example (see pages 102 and 116). The School Superior shares its hill site with the award-winning Benfica High School (designed by Raúl Hestnes Ferreira and Jorge Gouveia) which is already on the north-facing slope. The School Superior is surrounded by a dense urban area with six-to-seven-storey housing blocks and the recently remodelled motorway, Avenida General Norton de Matos. The large forest of the Parque de Monsanto is close by.

The building seems a moored ship as it stretches over the hill site while simultaneously emphasising and fortifying its boundary on the hill with the motorway below. It is a key building generating a new sense of place in the area. The composition is a display of overlapping elements, each manipulated in turn to create intricate volumes similar to those found in the paintings of the twentieth-century Dutch abstract painter Piet Mondrian.

Initially the School of Media Studies consisted of two blocks set in the slope: one tall with supporting services, the other lower and longer with classrooms above auditoriums, and studios.

The building's hill-top splendour is seen to best effect from its northern approach. The visitor is encouraged to approach the building by its outstretched elements and by a sinuous path of fragmented stones that leads up to and under the taller square block. At sunset this block appears as a large white canvas floating on several columns.

Once the building is approached, stairs become visible, seeming to disappear into the ground in the courtyard. On closer inspection the stairs reveal a passage into the bowels of the building where a cafeteria is situated, creating an intimate enclave. The colour of the interior creates a

Benfica

João Luís Carilho da Graça 1992–94

Benfica

João Luís Carilho da Graça 1992–94

distinctive sense of a public space with private enclaves. The white face of the building displays stairs and walkways that are often glazed or appear as open grooves in the concrete fabric. These stairs and walkways shield the classrooms from the expressway. Red is applied to walls that have classrooms or staff rooms behind them. This is seen especially in the courtyard were the occasional white surface penetrates a red wall to reveal the series of interconnections. The two blocks are divided by a glazed atrium and are linked by the walkways and stairs, creating a strong sense of theatre with a balcony and terraces between the public and private realms, which lend a sense of spectacle to the courtyard.

ADDRESS Rua Professor José Sebastião,
off Avenida General Norton de Matos [9G]
TRAIN Benfica
METRO Colégio Militar
BUS 16, 16C, 24, 29, 46, 54, 63, 67
ACCESS grounds only
Secil Prize 1994

Benfica

João Luís Carilho da Graça 1992–94

Benfica

João Luís Carilho da Graça 1992–94

Barrio do Bom Pastor

In 1994, the new government wanted a fresh approach to the age-old problem of rehousing the city's poor, especially those living in sheds normally constructed of sheets of corrugated iron or, more usually, of found materials. The Programa Especial de Realojamento proposed to eradicate completely the sheds still remaining after the initiatives of the previous Programa de Intervencao de Medio Prazo, and to relocate their inhabitants in the city itself rather than extraditing them to its periphery where the increasing population was expanding and the associated rise in poor housing was becoming difficult to control.

The Barrio do Bom Pastor is the first public housing development to be built under the Programa Especial de Realojamento. The site is triangular next to a railway line and is adjacent to a street. A rectilinear block adjoins four units. Each unit has 20 apartments, with apartment being of mixed use with three-to-five rooms. The block has a simple and smooth elevation that alternates between a warm yellow at the front to a crisp white at the rear.

The approach to the rear of the building, which also has vehicular access, is lined with trees that act as a screen to protect the inhabitants from the noise of railway line. The trees also shield the public courtyard which precedes a row of porches that lead from it to the ground-floor flats. This courtyard overlooks Parque Monsanto which provides an intimacy and human scale to the development. A delicate sequence of bridges leading from the main street to the blocks is an attempt at enclosing and removing the scheme from the immediacy of the nearby street.

Although the medium-rise development has a relatively high population density, the scheme manages to express aspects of both community life and individual privacy and freedom.

The scheme was originally designed to house a group of gypsies who

Ana Lucia Barbosa 1997

Ana Lucia Barbosa 1997

were living in squalid conditions in corrugated-metal shanty huts without sanitation. In the eyes of the State they are a group avoiding taxes. But the building has proved both popular and functional, and an identical scheme is being planned on the opposite side of the road.

ADDRESS Rua de Antonio Ferro, south off Avenida da Venezuela [9E]
CLIENT Departamento Construção de Habitação
SIZE 40 units
TRAIN Rossio to Benfica
BUS 109 only from Benfica railway station
ACCESS none, visible from the street

Benfica

Ana Lucia Barbosa 1997

Benfica

Ana Lucia Barbosa 1997

Colombo Centre

The Colombo Centre has had its share of attacks in the local press, not in terms of its pastiche architecture but for its failure to provide opportunties for the local workforce and for its poor conditions, all of which is helping to destroy this old residential district on Lisbon's periphery.

Associate architect J Quintela da Fonseca refers to the centre as 'A small city and not a large building'. This is near to the truth: the complex is the largest commercial centre in the Iberian peninsula with more than 410,000 square metres of floor space over three floors.

The building's design, like Expo, is based on a theme of the seas, though it is historical, paying homage to the Discoveries. It is adorned in steel-clad columns, the colour of which gives the illusion of being stone. Several glass and verdigris copper domes rest on top of the building like candles on a cake. Materials, which had to be maintenance-free, include granite and the Portuguese Calçada stone used for the traditional paving. A fabric membrane graces the roof of the Playcenter, which is literally an indoor fun fair-come-sports arena and a new concept in Portugal. However, architecturally the centre is an ostentatious chasm.

ADDRESS Avenida Lusiada [10H]
CLIENT Grupo Sonae Imobliaria – Ing. Real Estate International
ASSOCIATE ARCHITECT J Quintela da Fonseca
LANDSCAPE ARCHITECT Mahan Rykiel Associates
ENGINEER Prog+Fabril, SA
CONTRACT VALUE £241 million
SIZE 85,000 square metres total site area
METRO Colégio Militar-Luz
ACCESS 10.00–midnight

Benfica

RTKL Associates, Inc. 1994–97

RTKL Associates, Inc. 1994–97

Olaias to Olivais

Alto da Pina housing 186
Olaias complex, Altis Park Hotel 188
Bairro do Armador 192
Church of St Maximilio Kolbe 196
Santa Clara Chapel 198
Olivais Sul shopping centre 200

Alto da Pina housing

These subsidised flats make up the final phase of the Programa de Intervencao de Medio Prazo, a project devised in 1987 for the construction of around 9700 apartments on the city's periphery for residents then in temporary municipal accommodation and for those living in barracas, or squalid sheds. Many of Lisbon's housing schemes under the programme suffer from poor amenities and are situated far from any reasonable shopping district. However, the brief for this project stipulated that inhabitants were to be rehoused close to their previous surroundings to lessen their feeling of alienation and so that they would be close to the Olaias shopping centre and the nearby district of Areeiro.

The five-storey block consolidates the traditional street pattern, and is filled completely with the inhabitants from the nearby sheds formerly on the Rua Americo Durao. The building is amiably designed in yellow and terracotta, and contains a mix of accommodation in variously combined flats for three to five people. There are few balconies because the occupiers normally enclose them, ruining the original lines of the building and altering the concept of the architect.

ADDRESS Quinta do Monte Coxo, Rua Americo Durao, lots 1–6 off Avenida Afonso Costa [6Q]
CLIENT Departamento de Construção de Habitação
SIZE 63 units, nine commercial shops
METRO Arieiro or Olaias
BUS 40, 56 from Arieiro
ACCESS none, visible from the street

José Gomes Teixeira 1995

Olaias to Olivais

José Gomes Teixeira 1995

Olaias complex, Altis Park Hotel

The Olaias complex is still in progress more than 20 years after the initial concept. The initial phase was a commercial apartment terrace built in 1975 which won Tomás Taveira an award that inspired a succession of flamboyant buildings throughout Lisbon and the rest of Portugal, and as far afield as the Portuguese territory of Macao. The apartment terrace today is worn and tired-looking and in need of refurbishment. The luxurious apartments, with top-floor duplexes and underground parking, are an archetype for future developments in the area.

Since construction began, the site has developed to include three accommodation blocks, two office developments, a shopping centre, a private sports club and, its latest addition, the Altis Park Hotel. It is situated on a gently sloping hill that leads to an escarpment, recently connected by a bridge to the Vale de Chelas. This link now has views of the new metro below as it crosses a colourful mosaic-clad bridge between tunnels.

The complex sits between the Areeiro and Picheleira districts, and slight differences in its architectural language can be seen. The shopping centre is a linear structure entered through a decorated gateway off the avenue overlooking the Rotunda das Olaias. It also encloses a recent social-housing project, Barrio de Bom Pastor (see page 178).

The centre is followed by the pinnacle of the development, the hotel, which is a modern and comfortable glazed tower with 300 rooms and an international conference centre occupying a corner site facing both the river and Expo. At ground level it carries a strong, sweeping mix of red and green which conveys the usual Taveira iridescent colours. (These need a new coat of paint every couple of years to prevent them looking worn and aged.)

The hotel has slightly restrained architectural motifs, though some are

Tomás Taveira 1972–95

Tomás Taveira 1972–95

reminiscent of other projects such as the apartments opposite the Olaias club which have the same turrets as the Amoreiras complex (see page 88). Guests have exclusive use of the Olaias Club, again less adorned with pomo motifs but using geometries wildly, creating loud, confusing but exciting and well thought-out interiors.

ADDRESS Avenida Eng. Arantes e Oliveira, Olaias [6Q, 6R]
METRO Areeiro or Olaias
BUS 20 from Praça do Marques Pombal
ACCESS shopping centre and hotel only

Tomás Taveira 1972–95

Tomás Taveira 1972–95

Bairro do Armador

The years since the revolution of 1974 have witnessed the growth of shanty structures, or 'Barracas' around Lisbon. These house the various communities from Portugal's former colonies in Africa. Labyrinths of these illegal settlements have developed on valuable city land.

Now there is a campaign to demolish what are referred to as the slums of the city, the sheds made of sheets of corrugated iron or, more usually, of found materials. Most of the families from the slums have been rehoused in the unsavoury neighbourhood of Chelas. It has been constructed at breakneck speed and the design ignores what would normally be regarded as necessities for good community housing: for example, it has megastructures along small pavements, creating large differences in scale. The Bairro do Armador is one part of Chelas and is the municipality's latest venture in the property market where it builds and then sells housing, often to cooperatives. The designs are usually created in an alliance between the municipality and the cooperative's own architect.

The buildings are placed in a bland suburban zone that still does not have amenities close by. Most buildings remain isolated and are placed haphazardly in the suburban landscape, and this form of alienation is reflected in the antisocial behaviour of the diverse cultural groups rehoused here. For example, as most of the area is still under construction, children play in and around the building sites.

It is difficult to predict how Bairro do Armador will develop, but the future may be anticipated in one ten-storey building decorated with stripes of ochre and terracotta and which has unspoilt views across the river and the more luxurious Olaias complex beyond (see page 188).

The rehousing programme has done little to sustain the pride of the communities affected, despite the improvement made to living conditions

Helder Tério and Elias Rodrigues 1994–97

Helder Tério and Elias Rodrigues 1994–97

with, for instance, the provision of safe running water and electricity. In fact, the overcrowded community structure generates a degree of pessimism.

Olaias to Olivais

ADDRESS Bairro do Armador,
Azinhada Armador [6R]
CLIENT Departamento Construção
de Habitação
LANDSCAPE ARCHITECTS Paulo Gonçalves
and Maria João Ferreira
METRO Vale de Chelas BUS 59, 103
ACCESS none, visible from the street

Helder Tério and Elias Rodrigues 1994–97

Helder Tério and Elias Rodrigues 1994–97

Church of St Maximilio Kolbe

The church of St Maximilio Kolbe has been likened to an organ because of the tall blue–grey concrete cylinders which form its exterior walls. The terracotta-coloured roof can be seen from across the valley in Olaias, from where it seems to be a tower. Currently the church is intended to become an integral part of a housing estate to be built in the Bairros de Alfinetes and Condado regions, areas that have been growing ever since the development of social housing there in the 1970s. There is a growing trend of worship away from the city's cathedrals to local churches on the periphery and this is reflected in this church's ever-expanding congregation. To cope with the demand and to increase space, the church will have a chapel added once construction of the extra housing begins.

ADDRESS Bairro do Condado, Rua de Ovar, entrance through Avenida Paulo VI [6S]
CLIENT Patriarcado
LANDSCAPE ARCHITECT Maria João Ferreira
BUS 55, 59
ACCESS open

Pedro Vieira Almeida 1993

Pedro Vieira Almeida 1993

Santa Clara Chapel

The Santa Clara Chapel serves about 1660 families in a mixed neighbourhood of social housing schemes and cooperative developments. The chapel is the first phase of a much larger scheme that, once built, will reinforce the chapel's role in the community.

The building stands out on a hillside as a pristine, white form that almost seems like an apparition of an angel. A modest and simple geometric block is oversailed by an angled lid that shelters a small, airy prayer room from the sun. As a safety feature, the prayer room is fenced in by a gridded element. However the building as two functions: it has a chapel on top, with a community area below.

The main entrance to the north of the chapel is marked by a thin steel cross that is hardly visible. Inside, the materials used in construction are modest, simple and cheap. The chapel is filled with light and gives the interior a sense of spirituality, dignity and vitality; it is a modest sign of hope for the community and is a positive contribution to the fractured urban realm around it, a realm epitomised by the apprehensive-looking bridge nearby.

ADDRESS Avenida Avelino Teixeira de Mota [8R]
CLIENT Patriacado
METRO Vale de Chelas
BUS 59 from Areeiro
ACCESS Monday–Saturday 16.00–20.00, Sunday 08.30–12.00

Olaias to Olivais

Gonçalo Byrne 1996

Olaias to Olivais

Gonçalo Byrne 1996

Olivais Sul shopping centre

Olivais Sul shopping centre was built in a district without a main shopping area. It is surrounded by many houses built in the 1960s and looking almost like individual scattered towers among plentiful areas of greenery. The area's layout and its name, Olivais, meaning olive-yards, are reminders of a landscape which was planted with olive groves. The whole project is speculative and was created to rejuvenate a run-down area with very few, if any, amenities while taking advantage of the new infrastructure developments such as the underground links to Expo and the new bridge over the Tagus river.

The scheme has a shopping centre with four independent towers each occupying a corner of the centre. The cladding is mostly in limestone, which alternates between smooth and rough striations and merges with the salmon-coloured towers above, which themselves may be seen through the glazed atrium of the centre.

The visitor is led to a modest entrance by lines of olive trees, planted as a small reminder of the orchards which used to dominate the area, and once inside is met by an atrium lit brightly by daylight. An information counter is packed uncomfortably under the stairs. The atrium provides a reference point for the whole shopping trip.

The shopping area has a simple and sensible plan and lacks some of the poor decorative schemes normally associated with other complexes in the city. Detailing is kept simple, crisp and easy to clean. The stainless-steel handrails end abruptly, curving and stretching past their boundary only to curl into the floor.

The cinema complex is contained in its own area and is easily accessed from all points. Also, a roof terrace elsewhere creates a public quadrangle rarely found in the neighbourhood where the restaurants and cafés animate the area and provide a space for people to socialise. The roof is

Frederico Valsassina 1995

Frederico Valsassina 1995

also connected by aerial links to phase two of the shopping complex, which is currently being developed. Eventually the whole site will cover more than 236,000 square metres and will include leisure facilities, office suites and accommodation, creating a centre in its own right within this suburb.

Olaias to Olivais

ADDRESS Rua Cidade de Bissau [9T]
CLIENT Liscenter
SIZE 73,149 square metres
METRO Olivais Sul
BUS 21 from Campo Pequeno
ACCESS shopping centre only

Frederico Valsassina 1995

Frederico Valsassina 1995

Parque Expo

Parque Expo 98   206
Expo Information Centre   214
South Gate (Petrogal Cracking Tower)   218
Multiuse Pavilion   220
Oceanarium   224

Parque Expo 98

Expo 98 celebrates the 500th anniversary of Vasco da Gama's discovery of the sea route to India, which provides the theme for the exposition: 'The oceans – a heritage for the future'. Parque Expo has been less boisterous about the event than its predecessors and is determined that it will not be a slick vision of the future 'with sex appeal', but instead will be a relatively modest affair with a brighter and more optimistic outlook, both economically and ecologically.

Although Expo will exhibit the usual ingenious architecture usually prevalent at these events, Lisbon has also taken a different approach to the event. The competitive stages were mainly between native architects, with some of the larger projects in fact being awarded to international names. Some buildings (about 30 per cent) will have a short lifespan and will be removed after the event to make way for new commercial projects. The larger, more impressive cultural buildings will remain permanently on site to encourage visitors and to promote financial investment. In fact, initial real-estate sales have already exceeded expectations and give hope for the future. The building of Expo and its associated infrastructure will also allow Lisbon to bid for the Olympic Games, which until now has been virtually impossible – the old capital city, though rich in culture, suffered from a lack of the appropriate infrastructure, resources and accommodation necessary to stage such an internationally important event.

Expo will be sited to the north-east of the city on a 5-km riverside stretch on the Tagus that was once an industrial area. New infrastructural projects include a carriageway carried on a bridge spanning 15 kilometres, 10 of which will be over water. It will create a more direct route between Lisbon and the rest of the country to the north and south and is believed to have been built with foresight as the major route to Lisbon's

J V Rosa (master planner), Manuel Salgado (chief Expo planner) 1998

J V Rosa (master planner), Manuel Salgado (chief Expo planner)

second airport. There will also be a new railway station, designed by Santiago Calatrava, that will be the main entrance to the site, after which it will be the city's central and international station and linked with the new metro and airport not too far away. The site will also house the heating and cooling infrastructure for the district and will have an underground pneumatic waste disposal systems.

A protocol arrangement between Expo and the Centre for the Conservation of Energy 93 was agreed to make the most of the 'supermarket of natural energies'. Undoubtedly the plans were approved by the European Commission which provided assistance towards funding. With landscaping initiatives receiving the majority, less aid was given towards the construction of buildings, the only one to receive an award being the Utopian Pavilion.

The fair itself will be spread over 60 hectares. The Utopian Pavilion will be the biggest building on site with an auditorium with a capacity of 17,500 people It will be built using Glulam-laminated timber, which relates to the structure of a caravel or upturned boat Its interconnected halls will be naturally air conditioned using water taken from the river.

All national exhibits will be displayed within the Participating Countries Pavilion, designed by Alberto Barreiros Ferreira and Alberto França Dória, to ensure that the overall Expo theme is maintained. The pavilion will be home to the Lisbon Exhibition Centre after Expo. A series of linked international pavilions, large enough in total to contain 15 football pitches, will house each national stand. Other temporary and removable structures designed by RISCO – Manuel Salgado will be used for the same purpose, but placed around the south gate. The Portuguese will have a separate national stand, also designed by Alvaro Siza Vieira. It is an intriguing two-storey structure extravagantly clad in

J V Rosa (master planner), Manuel Salgado (chief Expo planner) 1998

J V Rosa (master planner), Manuel Salgado (chief Expo planner)

marble with a draping concrete canopy held by rods over the public square which will host the official ceremony. However, the most striking building will be the Oceanarium designed by the Peter Chermayeff of Cambridge Seven Associates, Inc. (page 224). Situated on an island at the centre of the Expo scheme, the Oceanarium has four stone towers surrounding a huge central tank, each tower displaying a different marine ecology and habitat. Glass canopies suspended on tall masts will provide shade.

Among the large exhibition buildings will be smaller facilities with themes such as youth and health centres, public and private schools, hospitals, and university institutes, interspersed between public spaces and shopping areas, a marina, and cafés and restaurants. There will also be residential and service areas of which only the north zone, where villa Expo is located, will be substantially built for the event. This zone merges with a large landscaped park and extends northwards under the new bridge. The idea of a new city park not only provides an environmental challenge but also adds to its success as an urban renewal development. The master plan by George Hargreaves and PROAP integrates landforms with hydrology and landfills, and cleans up one the most polluted rivers in Portugal, the Trancão. The site will be planted experimentally with shrubs and plants to test their adaptability to this difficult and challenging urban environment.

Initially, designated areas will provide parking for visitors during the event, but it is intended that the park will ultimately provide a safe area suitable for public events – avoiding the fate of the Parque de Montesanto which is now a haven for antisocial activities.

The long-term aim is to use Expo as a springboard for greater prosperity for the area in particular and Lisbon as a whole.

J V Rosa (master planner), Manuel Salgado (chief Expo planner) 1998

J V Rosa (master planner), Manuel Salgado (chief Expo planner)

BUILDINGS AND ARCHITECTS

Gare do Oriente train station: Santiago Calatrava

Oceanarium, Peter Chermayeff of Cambridge Seven Associates, Inc. (page 224)

Utopian Pavilion: Regino Cruz with Skidmore, Owings & Merrill, Inc. (page 220)

Participating Countries Pavilion: Alberto Barreiros Ferreira and Alberto França Dória

Portuguese Pavilion: Alvaro Siza Vieira (interior, Eduardo Souto Moura)

Expo HQ, Architecturo–Arqui III

MODULAR STRUCTURES

Expo Information Centre: Miguel Arruda (page 214)

Restaurants and installations: RISCO – Manuel Salgado

Knowledge of the Seas: João Luís Carilho da Graça

Video Stadium: Luisa Pacheco Marques

Unicef Pavilion: Alex Burmester

North Gate: Manuel Tainha

South Gate (Petrogal Cracking Tower): Manuel Graça Dias and José Egas Vieira (page 218)

ADDRESS Parque Expo 98

CONTRACT VALUE about £1.5–£2 billion

SIZE 350 hectares total regenerated area, 60 hectares Expo grounds

TRAIN Gare do Oriente

METRO Oriente

ACCESS 22 May–30 September 1998, 09.00–15.00 (for further information and the site map, see http://www.expo98.pt)

J V Rosa (master planner), Manuel Salgado (chief Expo planner) 1998

Parque Expo

Parque Expo

J V Rosa (master planner), Manuel Salgado (chief Expo planner)

Expo Information Centre

Antecedent to the opening of Expo, the Information Centre is situated at the southern end of the site and announces a new building type, while creating a stylish impression for first-time visitors. In fact its size, and functional and flexible metal structure whets the appetite for the rest of the exposition. The Centre began life as a temporary structure previously used for the 'Porto 1865 Uma Exposição' in Oporto in 1994. Its function here, however, is to house a series of exhibitions explaining to the public the World Fair scheme and theme, and the development of the Expo.

Distinguished by its unmistakable curved gleaming silver skin, the Information Centre makes no obvious concessions to any conventional building type but instead echoes the forms of ships passing by. The simplicity of the materials and form employed allows it to be seen from all angles while at the same time emphasising the direction of the exposition. The front façade is tilted inwards towards a pool set in a lawn to create a 'moat' around the building. The entrance faces the Tagus, which is reached by a pleasurable, winding path beside the pool, which momentarily reveals the exposition to the visitors.

It is hard escaping the Expo theme in the Centre. The blue floor is adorned with a multitude of fish that contrast with the timid, light-coloured timber of the reception and cloakroom counters, which have an ephemeral quality about them. A refreshments bar shares the ground floor with an extension built on a wood-decked concrete platform from where visitors can relax and enjoy the view across the river.

Arranged over four levels, interconnected by fair-faced concrete stairs (an element that detracts from its ephemerality), and expressing the full height of its structural frame, this void discloses a triple-height of exhibition spaces, offices and an auditorium. The positioning of the stairs is

Miguel Arruda 1997

Parque Expo

Miguel Arruda 1997

emphasised by a cut in the entrance wall, leads the visitor to a protected balcony, again providing a dramatic and panoramic view of site and river.

The building had a disastrous start with wood panels dropping off ceilings while the curved skin had to be restructured to withstand the strong winds that characterise this part of Lisbon.

Parque Expo

ADDRESS Avenida Marechal Gomes da Costa
CLIENT Parque Expo 98, SA
LANDSCAPE ARCHITECT G Ribeiro Telles
BUS 18, 25, 25A
ACCESS open

Miguel Arruda 1997

South Gate (Petrogal Cracking Tower)

Cracking Tower, which is an isolated object set in the landscape, is in reality Expo's South Gate and is a reminder of the site's history when it housed a distillery for Petrogal, a petroleum company. The newly renovated tower will have a café and will provide panoramic views over the entire Expo site and river. The beacon will be encircled by a ramp encased in translucent glass leading to a round balcony above. At night, the pedestrianised route will create a sinuous glow of fluorescent light and will act as a focal point for that part of the site. Besides the green-coloured tower, the gatehouse, an angular-shaped vessel-like structure housing services and the ticket office, will exist alongside a string of trees. Fortunately, the tower will remain after Expo, but the vessel-like structure will not.

Parque Expo

ADDRESS Praça da Torre de Cracking
CLIENT Parque Expo 98, SA
ARTIST Pedro Calapez
BUS 18, 25
ACCESS open

Manuel Graça Dias and Egas José Vieira 1994–98

Parque Expo

Manuel Graça Dias and Egas José Vieira 1994–98

Multiuse Pavilion

The Multiuse Pavilion will also be named the Utopian Pavilion during Expo and will be – according to the local newspapers – the jewel in the Expo crown, mainly because of its ecological significance (which attracted grants from the European Community). It will be the largest covered stadium in the country with a capacity of 17,500 people.

The pavilion's design is based on the concept of an overturned caravel, and relates particularly to Vasco da Gama's ship used to journey out of the Tagus to discover the world five centuries ago. Inevitably the plans relate to the hull, incorporating concurrent halls that are interconnected to provide flexible and utilitarian facilities. The pavilion has the capacity to transform its interior to suit a multitude of cultural and sporting events, from stage shows to boxing and windsurfing.

The scheme pushes gently and humanely at the edges of 'green' issues as well as new technologies. The structure is the result of an overt design strategy, aiming for environmentally friendly construction and overall energy efficiency. The air is ventilated and cooled naturally by the river which reduces the need for air-conditioning by about 40 per cent. This amounts to a global reduction in energy costs of up to 80 per cent compared with other traditional buildings. The roof is the pavilion's main feature and has a smooth silver skin supported by Glulam-laminated timber trusses that span 114 metres, and adjustable louvres, are operated by photocells, that control the amount of daylight onthe surface of the structure.

It is no surprise to find that the Multiuse Pavilion has been given the Energy Comfort 2000 award by the European Commission Thermie Project on account of its energy-efficiency capabilities. Practically a spectre of The Dome of Discovery Pavilion by Ralph Tubbs that dominated the 1951 Festival of Britain in London, the Multiuse Pavilion

Regino Cruz with Skidmore, Owings & Merrill, Inc. 1996–98

Regino Cruz with Skidmore, Owings & Merrill, Inc. 1996–98

fortunately will not follow the same fate as its counterpart and should remain on the Expo site for the staging of a future Olympic event.

ADDRESS Parque Expo 98
CLIENT Parque Expo 98, SA
STRUCTURAL ENGINEERS Skidmore, Owings & Merrill, Inc. and J L Câncio Martins
CONSULTING ENGINEERS MEDA & LM
CONTRACT VALUE £35 million
SIZE 41,118 square metres (maximum of 17,500 seats)
METRO Oriente
ACCESS open

Regino Cruz with Skidmore, Owings & Merrill, Inc. 1996–98

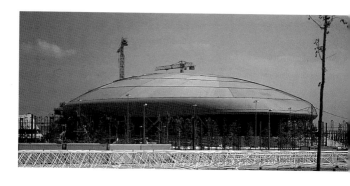

Parque Expo

Regino Cruz with Skidmore, Owings & Merrill, Inc. 1996–98

Oceanarium

Portugal has been a conservative nation, but with Expo 98 it has vigorously embraced modern architecture of many shapes and sizes. The Oceanarium or Ocean Pavilion is the largest aquarium in the world. Because of its important role at Expo it was granted its own site at the quay of the Docas dos Olivais, an island of its own which evokes the image of a ship. The pavilion has no overt orientation but has a central mass rising from the water with towers at all four corners. Each tower has textured stone walls with glass inserts, while above is an undulating glass roof held by steel masts and tension cables. This device creates a transition from the scale of the Expo to the openness of the busy harbour with its many boats.

The pavilion's point of entry is from a second, land-bound building linked by a bridge with two levels, the upper for entering and the lower for exiting. The block also contains offices, a shop and a temporary exhibition hall. The entrance building's wall is enriched with an array of blue glazed tiles conveying images of aquatic wildlife. It was created in the image of computer pixels and is in keeping with the Portuguese tradition of *azulejo* tiles. Unfortunately, the wall is semi-covered, its splendour best seen from a distance.

Inside, the aquarium consists of a large, central tank for fish viewed from two, dark levels and an underwater access point. The tank is linked to the adjoining four habitats – each with various species of birds and fish – in each of the pavilion's towers by three means: bridges or balconies above, acrylic panels below, and by underwater passages. These corner enclosures are brightly lit by natural light and create amazing long, diagonal views. There are other smaller tanks and rooms for exhibitions at lower levels.

The building's form and structure are awe-inspiring, the gathered

Cambridge Seven Associates, Inc. 1997

Cambridge Seven Associates, Inc. 1997

geometries forming a new icon for the city. This will be the most spectacular and attractive building at Expo and is likely to remain so for years to come.

Parque Expo

ADDRESS Docas dos Olivas
CLIENT Parque Expo 98, SA
ASSOCIATE ARCHITECTS Promontorio
Arquitectos Associados, LDA
ENGINEERS Ove Arup & Partners
International
COST £40 million
ACCESS open

Cambridge Seven Associates, Inc. 1997

Cambridge Seven Associates, Inc. 1997

Index

Alges bus station **108–110**
Alif Hotel **142**
Altis Park Hotel 188
Alto da Ajuda 116
Alto da Pina housing **186**
Amoreiras complex **88–90**
Ana Salazar shop **30–32**
Ângelo Silva, Miguel
  Espaço OIKOS **26–28**
Anna Molinari shop **78**
Archaeological Nucleus Museum
  22–24
Architecturo–Arqui III 212
Arpad Szenes–Vieira da Silva Foundation
  94–96
Arquitectos, LDA
  Doca do Santo bar **118**
  Doca Louca, news kiosk and bar **124**
Arruda, Miguel 212
  Expo Information Centre **214–216**
Atalaia 31 shop **38**
Aurelio, José 66
Avenidas Novas 134

Bairro Alto 38
Bairro Arco do Cego **146**
Bairro do Armador **192–194**
Bairro do Condado 196
Bandarra shoe shop **18**
BANIF bank **168**
Bank National Ultramarino **138**
Barbosa, Ana Lucia
  Barrio do Bom Pastor **178–180**
Barreiros Ferreira, Alberto 208, 212
Barrio do Bom Pastor **178–180**

Belém cultural centre **112–114**
Benfica High School 174
Bimotor Records **58**
Bofill, Ricardo 9
Branco,Casino
  Eden Aparthotel **60**
Brandão, Augusto
  School of Architecture, Technical
    University of Lisbon 116
Building Design Partnership 9
Burmester, Alex 212
Byrne, Gonçalo 8
  Dona Maria II National Theatre,
    bookshop, bar and ticket office **14–16**
  Santa Clara Chapel **198**

Café da Ponte **120–122**
Café Targus **40**
Caixa Geral de Depositos **144–146**
Calatrava, Santiago 212
Calouste Gulbenkian Foundation
  Headquarters 136
Cambridge Seven Associates, Inc. 210,
  212
  Oceanarium **224–226**
Campolide 102
Câncio Martins, J L 222
Cardoso, Arsénio
  Torre do Tombo 154
Cargalheiro, Manuel
  Cidade Universitária metro entrance
    158
Carilho da Graça, João Luís 212
  School Superior de Comunicação Social
    174–176

Casanostra restaurant **42**
Castelo Sao Jorge 154
Castle de São Jorge 26
Castro & Melo building **34–36**
Chelas 192
Chermayeff, Peter 210, 212
Chiado National Gallery 48
Chiado restructuring 9, **34–36**
Chicó, Henrique
Heron Castillo building **68**
Church of St Maximilio Kolbe **196**
Cidade Universitária metro entrance
158
Club VII **84**
Colombo Centre **182**
Consenso restaurant **46**
Cordeiro, Arsénio Raposo
Caixa Geral de Depositos **144–146**
Coreto da Liberdade **82**
Costa, Daciano 114
Cruz, Regino 212
Avenida Duque de Avila, 185 **134**
Multiuse Pavilion **220–222**

da Silva Pinheiro, Coelho
Victoria building **64**
da Silva, Vieira 94
de Carvalho Blanc, Cristina B S
St José Psychiatric Clinic **172**
de Carvalho, Fernão L S
St José Psychiatric Clinic **172**
Din, Rashid
Fashion Clinic **70**
Doca de Santo Amaro 118, 122, 124
Doca do Santo bar **118**

Doca Louca, news kiosk and bar **124**
Dona Maria II National Theatre
bookshop, bar and ticket office
14–16
dos Santos, Eugenio 22

Eden Aparthotel **60**
Edificio Alto das Amoreiras **92**
Egas Vieira, José 212
Elias Rodrigues
Bairro do Armador **192–194**
Espaço οιкοs **26–28**
Executive Inn Hotel **136**
Expo 98 7, 72, 114, 206–226
Expo HQ 212
Expo Information Centre 212, **214–216**

Faculty of Veterinary Sciences 8
Fashion Clinic
Fernanda Lamelas, Maria
Bimotor Records **58**
Fernandes, Rodrigues
Edificio Alto das Amoreiras **92**
Ferreira, António
Torre do Tombo **154**
Ferreira, J M D
Patio da Bagatella **98–100**
França Dória, Alberto 208, 212

Gare do Oriente train station 212
Gouveia, Jorge 174
Graça Dias, Manuel 212
Ana Salazar shop **30–32**
Casanostra restaurant **42**
South Gate **218**

Gregotti, Vittorio
  Belém cultural centre **112–114**
Guedes de Amorin, Carlos
  Tranquilidade Vida building **66**
Guterres, Antonio 7

Heron Castillo building **68**
Hestnes Ferreira, Raúl 174
  ISCTE library **164**

i Kiosk **20**
Institute of Management and Economy
  8
Intergaup
  Archaeological Nucleus Museum
    22–24
ISCTE library **164**

João Ferreira, Maria 196
Jorge Silva, Filipe
  Santo Condestável apartments **126**
José Vieira, Egas
  Ana Salazar shop **30–32**
  Casanostra restaurant **42**
  South Gate **218**

Kay, Sua
  BANIF bank **168**
Knowledge of the Seas 212

Lagarto, Antonio
  Atalaia 31 shop **38**
Larus, LDA 20
Lefor, Didier
  Executive Inn Hotel **136**

Lima Soares, Eduardo
  Post Office **62**
Lisboa Towers **170**
Lisbon Exhibition Centre 208
Lugero de Castro, Paulo
  Consenso restaurant **46**

Mahan Rykiel Associates 182
Manuel von Half, Maria
  Café Targus **40**
Marques, Carlos
  Alges bus station **108–110**
  Club VII **84**
Martin, Sir Leslie 136
Meira, Antonio
  Patine shop **44**
Metro City 8
Moleirinho, Jorge
  i Kiosk **20**
Mosteiro dos Jeronimos 112
Multiuse Pavilion **220–222**
Museum of Contemporary Art **48–50**

North Gate 212
Nova Campolide 102
Nuno Beitão, J
  Bandarra shoe shop **18**

Oceanarium 210, 212, **224–226**
Offices at Avenida Duque de Avila, 185
  134
Olaias complex, Altis Park Hotel **188–190**
Olivais Sul shopping centre **200–202**
Orfão, Rul
  Café da Ponte **120–122**

Ove Arup & Partners International 226

Pacheco Marques, Luisa 212
Parque de Monsanto 174
Parque Eduardo VII 9, 80, 82, 84
    Public lavatories **80**
Parque Expo 98 **206–210**
Parque Florestal de Monsanto 116
Parque Monsanto 178
Participating Countries Pavilion 208,
    212
Patine shop **44**
Patio da Bagatella **98–100**
Pedro Cabrita, Rui
    Espaço OIKOS **26–28**
Pencreac'h, G
    Eden Aparthotel **60**
Peri, Shay
    Anna Molinari shop **78**
Petrogal Cracking Tower, see South
    Gate
Pharmacy Faculty library **160**
Pinto Rocha, Luis Miguel 62
Portuguese Architects Association
    52–54
Portuguese Commercial Bank 22
Portuguese Pavilion 212
Post Office **62**
Prog+Fabril, SA 182
Programa de Intervencao de Medio Prazo
    186
Promontorio Arquitectos Associados, LDA
    226
Psychology and Education Sciences
    Faculty 156

Quimarães, Joaquim
    Parque Eduardo VII public lavatories
    80
Quintela da Fonseca, J 182
Quitanilha, Olga
    Santo Condestável apartments **126**

Ribeiro Telles, G 216
RISCO 114, 212, 208
Roque, Carlos
    Coreto da Liberdade **82**
Rosa, José V
    Parque Expo 98 206
Rotunda I metro station **72–74**
Rotunda II metro station **76**
RTKL Associates, Inc.
    Colombo Centre **182**

St José Psychiatric Clinic **172**
Salgado, Manuel 114, 208, 212
    Parque Expo 98 **206**
Santa Clara Chapel **198**
Santa-Rita, João
    Rotunda I metro station **72–74**
Santa-Rita, José
    Rotunda I metro station **72–74**
Santo Condestável apartments **126**
Santos Reis church extension **152**
School of Architecture, Technical
    University of Lisbon **116**
School Superior de Comunicação Social
    174–176
Secil Architectural Prize 9
Segadaes Tavares Associados, LDA 36,
    114

Serpa, Safira
    Stivali shoe shop **148**
Sete Rios 168
Simões, Duarte
    Rotunda II metro station **76**
Simões, Nuno
    Rotunda II metro station **76**
Siza Vieira, Alvaro 8, 208, 212
    Chiado restructuring **34–36**
Skidmore, Owings & Merrill, Inc. 212
    Multiuse Pavilion **220–222**
Soledade Sousa, Mario
    Café Targus **40**
Sommer Ribeiro, José
    Arpad Szenes–Vieira da Silva
    Foundation **94–96**
South Gate 212, **218**
Souto Moura, Eduardo 212
Souza, M A
    Patio da Bagatella **98–100**
Stivali shoe shop **148**
Streets, etc
    Alameda da Universidade 154, 156
    Avenida Afonso Costa 186
    Avenida Avelino Teixeira de Mota 198
    Avenida Caloste Gulbenkian 102
    Avenida Cardeal Cerejeira 84
    Avenida Conde Valbom 136
    Avenida da Liberdade 64, 66, 68, 70
    Avenida da Venezuela 180
    Avenida do Brazil 152
    Avenida Duque de Avila 134
    Avenida Eng. Arantes e Oliveira 190
    Avenida Eng. Duarte Pacheco 90
    Avenida 5 de Outubro 140

Avenida Forças Armadas 164
Avenida General de Matos 170
Avenida General Norton de Matos 176
Avenida Joao XXI 144, 146, 148
Avenida José Malhoa 168
Avenida Lusiada 182
Avenida Marechal Gomes da Costa 216
Avenida Professor Gamma Pinto 158,
    160, 162
Campo Grande 152
Campo Pequeno 142
Praça D Manuel 110
Praça D Pedro IV 16
Praça da Torre de Cracking 218
Praça das Amoreiras 94, 96
Praça do Imperio 114
Praça do Marques Pombal 70, 74, 76,
    80
Praça dos Restauradores 58, 60, 62
Quinta da Torre do Fato 172
Rua A Albino Machado 170
Rua Americo Durao 186
Rua Arco do Cego 146
Rua Artilharia 100
Rua Augusta 20
Rua Augusto Rosa 28
Rua Azedo Gneco 126
Rua Braamcamp 68
Rua Castilho 82
Rua Cidade de Bissau 202
Rua D João V 92
Rua da Academia das Ciencias 46
Rua da Atalaia 38
Rua de Antonio Ferro 180
Rua de Campolide 104

Streets, etc (continued)
  Rua de Ovar 196
  Rua Delfim de Brito Guimarães 168
  Rua Diario Noticias 40
  Rua dos Correeiros 24
  Rua Eng. Vieira da Silva 132
  Rua J Gomes Ferreira 92
  Rua Joaquim Antonio Aguiar 78
  Rua Nova da Almada 32, 36
  Rua Professor José Sebastião 176
  Rua San Filipe Nery 98
  Rua Sta Justa 18
  Rua Serpa Pinto 50
  Rua Tomás da Fonseca 170
  Travessa Água da Flor 44
  Travessa do Poço da Cidade 42
  Travessa Estevão Pinto 104
Swimming pool **162**
Szenes, Arpad 94

Tainha, Manuel 212
  Psychology and Education Sciences
    Faculty **156**
  Universidade Nova, canteen and
    dormitory **102–104**
Tamm, Carlos
  Alif Hotel **142**
Taveira, Tomás 8
  Amoreiras complex **88–90**
  Bank National Ultramarino **138**
  Olaias complex, Altis Park Hotel
    188–190
Teixeira, José Gomes
  Alto da Pina housing **186**
Telheiras 170, 172

Tério, Helder
  Bairro do Armador **192–194**
Torre do Tombo **154**
Tranquilidade Vida building **66**
Tubbs, Ralph 220
25 de Abril bridge 8

Unicef Pavilion 212
Universidade Nova, canteen and
  dormitory **102–104**
Utopian Pavilion 212

Valsassina, Frederico
  Eden Aparthotel 60
  Lisboa Towers **170**
  Olivais Sul shopping centre **200–202**
  Santos Reis church extension **152**
  Swimming pool **162**
Vasco da Gama bridge 8
Vasconcelos, João
  Club VII **84**
Victoria building **64**
Video Stadium 212
Vieira Almeida, Pedro
  Church of St Maximilio Kolbe **196**
Vieira da Silva, Maria Helena 158
Virgin Megastore 60

Wilmotte, Jean-Michel
  Museum of Contemporary Art **48–50**

Lisbon: a guide to recent architecture